How to Cook a Deer... and Other Critters

A Game Cookbook for Men

by

Jim Hayes

A *Virginia Country* Magazine Publication

How to Cook a Deer...and Other Critters
by
Jim Hayes

Publisher
Garrison Ellis

Editor
Don Carl Steffen

Production
Lisa Cain Curran
Sondra W. Peek

Illustrations
Susan Caumont Escher

Design
DCS Enterprises, Ltd.

Financial Officer
Christopher M. Curran

A *Virginia Country* Magazine Publication

COUNTRY PUBLISHERS, INC.
113 E. Main St.
Berryville, VA 22611

All material from *The Art of Eating* by M.F.K. Fisher
reprinted with permission of Macmillan Publishing Company.
Copyright 1937, 1941, 1942, 1943, 1948, 1949, 1954, by M.F.K. Fisher, renewed
©1971, 1976, 1977, by Mary Kennedy Friede.

Material from *With Bold Knife & Fork*, by M.F.K.Fisher,
reprinted with permission of the Putnam Publishing Group.
©1968, 1969 by M.F.K. Fisher

All recipes from GAME COOKBOOK, by Charles E. Stuart, reprinted with
permission of Country Publishers.
© 1982 by The Country Publishers, Inc.

All rights reserved to How to Cook a Deer...and Other Critters.
Copyright ©1991 by James J. Hayes

Contents

Introduction 10

About Wine 14

About Spices, More or Less 16

Gravy, It can Make or Break You 20

Preparing The Meat 23

Equipment 27

On Being Camp Cook 30

Meal Planning 31

Shopping 33

Cooking 35

Big Game 40

Upland Game—Bunnies and Birds 79

Fish 112

Stews, Soups, and Chowders 126

Innards, Variety Meats, Miscellaneous Stuff 145

Some Tips on Leftovers 152

*For Tom Mayes, Ted Rodgers, and Donnie,
who would have understood;
and for B.G., who does.
Semper Fideles!*

DEDICATION

No one in America has written better about food than M.F.K. Fisher. For more than 50 years this remarkable lady has written eloquently and passionately about preparing, cooking, and serving food; about eating and drinking, and about the intricate relationships that exist between and among all man's basic hungers.

Poet, philosopher, scholar, and lover of life's bountiful pleasures, Mrs. Fisher is truly America's Grand Dame of Gastronomy.

Mary Frances Kennedy Fisher, this book is dedicated, with humility, love, and deep appreciation, to you, and to that bold spirit which is so uniquely yours.

J.J.H.
Evergreen, Colorado
July 4, 1991

*There is a communion of more than our bodies
when bread is broken
and wine is drunk.*

M.F.K. Fisher
The Art of Eating

INTRODUCTION

This book is about cooking deer meat and other fruits of the hunt. It is also about being camp cook, an odious chore for some, a source of pride and great pleasure for others. It's about something else, too.

I've always thought that more than one of man's basic appetites is satisfied when game, well and fairly taken, is prepared with care, served forth with some pride, and shared with loved ones and good companions. As M.F.K. Fisher, the grand lady to whom this book is dedicated, has noted more than once, there is a communion shared during such gustatory experiences that is about more than breaking bread and drinking wine. This book is also about that.

As I get closer to collecting Social Security than I care to think about, and look back on more than 40 years of hunting, fishing, camping and cooking, I realize that I have accumulated a great treasure trove of experiences that have enriched my life and nourished my soul.

I realize too, that I have met and loved some truly remarkable people. Some were city folks and businessmen, for whom the annual hunting trip was a much anticipated—then fondly remembered—escape from the tepid joys of city life. Others were farmers, ranchers, loggers, innkeepers, electricians, carpenters, and plumbers...country people, at home in the outdoors, and happy for the chance to stock the larder with fresh game. Some were uncomplicated; some were characters. All were well-worth knowing. They too, have enriched my life, and provided me with many wonderful memories.

From time to time throughout the book, I'll share some of those experiences and memories with you. I hope you enjoy them. If nothing else, they will serve to break up long strings of recipes.

Let me state right off the bat that I am by no means a *chef*, much less a *gourmet* chef. But I'm a passably good cook, experienced, if not highly skilled. To be sure, I have screwed up more than one game dinner in my chequered career in the kitchen.

Most often that happened because I over-spiced or overcooked the meat or fish of the day. (Less is definitely more when cooking game.) But I seem to have learned by doing, and believe I can present recipes, ideas, and advice that will make sense to the veteran cook, prevent the neophyte from making the same mistakes I did, and please the senses of both.

This book is written for men. I know that there are many fine sportswomen, hunters and fishermen - er, fisher*women*, out there. But being women, most of them already *know* how to cook, learning at their mothers' knees. They know by experience, what cut of meat is better braised than dry roasted, how to make a white sauce, and how to cook rice without making it a sodden, sticky mess. In my experience, most men don't.

When pressed, men are apt to say, "Hell yes, I know my way around a kitchen," and with a daring show of nonchalance, proceed to burn the coffee, serve eggs over easy like hockey pucks, and put to table a pair of once fine mallards that are now both burnt beyond recognition and bloody at the same time.

This book is for them, to help them complete the circle, to help them prepare and serve the game they have brought home from brook, field, or forest. For the hunter that can be a soul-satisfying experience, lifting him above the common perception of the hunter as some kind of foul-mouthed, cigar-chomping Bambi murderer, and restoring him to the once more commonly held and honorable position of provider of food for table.

Besides, there are many men whose wives or significant others refuse to cook, eat, or even look at fresh-killed game. I know, I was married to one of them once. For a lot of reasons, it's best to know how to cook game yourself.

Inside you'll find a section about the responsibilities and joys of being camp cook, about meal-planning and shopping, and about divvying up the work. (The cook does *not* do KP!) There's some talk about wine, both for drinking and cooking with, and some sage (?) advice about spices. There are discussions about cooking equipment; pots, pans, and stoves; and some easy ways to make good gravies.

What you won't find are any recipes that call for sauces;

white, Bérnaise, Béchamel, Escoffier, or any other kind. Most of them are time-consuming and fussy to make, and are a general pain in the ass. You have enough to do to get the hot meat and veggies out in good order without having the Hollandaise curdle. If you really want to know about sauces, I recommend the venerable *Joy of Cooking*, by the equally venerable Mrs. Rombauer. There are more than 130 sauce recipes in there, and it's probably the best all-around cookbook in America.

I make only two basic assumptions; that the reader is just that...that he can read well enough to follow directions, and that he gives enough of a damn about the end result to make the effort.

So, if you are somewhere between being a complete dunderhead in the kitchen and a *cuisinier chef,* read on. There is something here for you. The recipes are tried and true, the advice reasonably sound, and the opinions not overly outrageous, although they obviously reflect my own likes and prejudices. And the stories are true, too; or anyway, almost.

Have fun. Like so many other things in life, if cooking isn't fun, then I say it's spinach, and I say the hell with it.

...with good friends...and good food on the board,
and good wine in the pitcher,
we may well ask,
When shall we live if not now?

M.F.K. Fisher
The Art of Eating

ABOUT WINE

Saint Paul is supposed to have said, "Take a little wine for thy stomach's sake." If he didn't say it, he should have; it's not a bad idea. A bit of the grape before the fire, a sip of fine sour mash to warm you after a day in the numbing cold, an icy martini, shaken *or* stirred, before dinner...all have contributed their fair share to the "mellowing out" that is part of what a hunting camp is all about. Needless to say, moderation in all things, gentlemen, and even then, **ONLY** when all firearms have been carefully unloaded and put securely away for the night.

Wine is a great accompaniment to game meals, and though there are no hard and fast rules anymore, reds generally go better with meat and dark-fleshed birds, and whites go better with most other game birds, most fish, and even rabbits.

A generous splash of hearty burgundy, zinfandel, or Chianti can turn a plain old stew into something zesty and mouthwatering, and many of the recipes in here call for wine in the cooking process; also sometimes Cognac, bourbon, or beer. Frankly, none of the above-mentioned has ever been in short supply in any hunting camp I've ever been in, thank God.

Aside from the stews, the reds are good in and with roasts and pot roasts of deer, elk, bear, moose, and their attendant gravies. Whites are best in and with fish, such as trout and salmon, white meat birds like grouse and quail, as well as in many soups and gravies.

You don't need to buy expensive, vintage wines. But as Cajun chef and funnyman Justin Wilson said, "If it ain't good enough to drink, don' cook wit it!"

California jug wines will do nicely for both cooking and drinking. Among those I've found—to use Mrs. Fisher's term—*honest*, and good company in camp or kitchen, are Robert Mondavi Cabernet Sauvignon, August Sebatiani Zinfandel and Mountain Burgundy, Carlo Rossi Burgundy and Chianti, and Guild Vino da Tavola, if you can still find it anyplace. Chablis, Chardonnays and Rhine Wines from the same vineyards are all acceptable whites at modest prices...well under $10 a jug. Gallo Hearty Burgundy and Chablis are also quite good and fairly priced. I've found some of these on sale for as little as $6.49 a half-gallon, or whatever they call it these days. (I'm too old to mess with metrics!)

There are trendier vineyards with arty labels like Stag's Crotch and Virgin's Leap, and what have you, that may or may not be better, but they are certainly pricier, and most of them are not in the jug wine market.

And, don't forget the hard stuff. A splash of John Jameson's to flame your peppered elk steak, a dollop of sherry in your venison kidneys with button mushrooms, or a slosh of Grand Marnier in your duck with orange sauce will never hurt you. And have a little yourself while you're at it; it makes the cooking process flow smoothly. Of course, if you hit it too hard, the fine print in the recipes gets a little hard to read. But by all means, don't be afraid to cook with alcohol. Everyone will think you know what you're doing, and that's how reputations are made.

ABOUT SPICES, MORE OR LESS

Every recipe in this book calls for the use of one or more spices, and although any recipe should be a precise guide to achieving a desired result—the same result each time—spices are (forgive me) a matter of taste. Through experiment you'll find you like more or less of any given spice. Go for it! Cooking is a creative art, not a precise science.

Be warned, however, some spices are much stronger than others, and if a pinch of oregano is good, two pinches do not automatically make it better. If you want to increase the amount of spice in a recipe, do it gradually, and in small amounts. I like a sage stuffing in turkey, but found out the hard way that too much sage can make it inedible.

I've tried to make the recipes in here, mine and others', consistent in terms of measurement, and for small amounts I use the term "pinch." A pinch is what you can conveniently hold between your thumb and forefinger, and usually measures between 1/8 and 1/4 of a teaspoon. If you have a hand that dwarfs a catcher's mitt, use some discretion.

We are also talking here about dried spices, bottled or tinned. If you have fresh spices available, such as parsley, basil, mint, oregano, etc., wonderful; but you'll find them weaker than the dried, and may want to increase the amount you use.

Likewise, if you have a pepper mill, freshly-cracked pepper is wonderful on salads, baked potatoes and the like; but again, it's probably stronger than the pulverized pepper you put in a regular shaker, so be careful.

Over-salting has ruined more good meals than I can count. The people you are feeding can always add salt to suit their taste; but if you over-salt in the cooking, it's easy to end up with something that *nobody* can eat. Salt lightly while cooking.

I've spent most of my adult life being married to women of Italian background and heritage, and have developed both a taste and a high tolerance for such spices as oregano, sweet basil, and garlic...especially garlic. I use it generously in pot roasts, stews, salads and the like. Not only are such dishes improved by it's use, but it also kills cold and flu germs, stimulates virility, and keeps vampires from biting you in the neck. It will also make you smell like a goat.

Like anything else that grows, garlic is frequently inconsistent in size and strength. Some cloves are little bitty things about the size of the nail on your pinky finger, and strong as hell. I've seen others about the size of a Concord grape, and surprisingly mild. If a recipe calls for 2 or 3 cloves of garlic, it means medium-sized, medium-strength ones. Adjust up or down accordingly.

Most people find it unpleasant to bite into a hunk of garlic found in a stew or pot roast. Either mince it as fine as possible, mash it into a paste with a mortar and pestle (or bowl and spoon), or put it in the pot peeled, but whole, with a toothpick in it, so it can be fished out, or at least identified and thus, avoided.

If a recipe calls for a spice you don't have, don't worry about it. Obviously you can't make curried rabbit without curry, but in most cases the absence of one spice or another won't be missed. Some recipes call for minced shallots. These are neither onions, nor are they garlic, but they have some of the taste characteristics of both. A small yellow or white onion, or a couple of scallions (sometimes called spring or green onions) chopped up fine make a passable substitute.

Juniper berries are a great addition to many roast and stew recipes for game, and a lot of the recipes in here call for their use. If you've ever hunted in the early fall where junipers grow, you've probably seen the bright blue berries, especially on young trees. I usually pick a handful of them to munch on instead of smoking while walking the woods. They are sweetish tasting, smelling faintly of gin. Most of the major spice producers sell them dried and bottled, at which point they have lost their bright blue color and look like peppercorns. Ask your friendly supermarket manager to order them for you if you don't see them on the shelf.

If for some reason I was limited to the number of tins of spice I could get into the pocket of my hunting jacket, (the front, not the game pocket), I'd have to include peppercorns, both black and green, salt, parsley, basil, thyme, oregano, cracked red pepper, sage, bay leaves, Tabasco, Worcestershire, juniper berries, whole cloves, dried minced onions, chili powder, cumin, caraway seeds and fresh garlic. Your list will probably be different, and that's as it should be.

As I punned earlier, spices are a matter of taste.

I was 28 or so, back in the fall of 1960 when I first met John Schwanneger, sportsman, hunter, fly-fisherman, and owner of the Beaverkill Country Lodge, outside Roscoe in New York's Catskill Mountains. With the main house and a couple of outbuildings, the place could accomodate 12 to 15 hunters or fishermen, and sat on a hundred acres of prime deer country. It also had nearly a half mile of frontage on the Beaverkill River, one of the best trout streams east of the Mississippi.

John was about 55 at the time, with a little pot belly, a big nose and cigar to match, a great sense of humor, and the thickest German accent I ever heard outside of a war movie. I was there with Jim Brown, my friend and boss at the Madison Avenue ad agency where I worked then.

We had stopped at a watering hole near Middletown, which became a favorite over the years, for a couple of martinis, a thick steak and a few Irish coffees, arriving at the Lodge close to 10 o'clock, only slightly the worse for wear.

"Chim Bwown! By Chimminy, I'm glad to see you. Und ziss must be Shimmy Hace. I'm gonna call you Shimmy, because mit two Chim's, I vould get all zer time confused." And that was my introduction to this remarkable, lovely man, whom I would come to admire greatly over the years. It's hard to reproduce his accent in type; but it was sort of guttural, with great, rolling "R's," with lots of "Mits, instead of "Withs," "V's for "W's," and all the time you had the sneaking suspicion that he was pulling your leg.

We were joined at breakfast by John Conway, like Jim Brown, a regular at the lodge. Conway owned a string of funeral parlors in Jackson Heights and had a lot of money. Everything he had—hat, boots, brush pants, jacket, and gun—was brand new from Abercrombie & Fitch. I really felt like a bum in my beat up field jacket from Sears, and a pair of old jeans. Worse, I had hocked my shotguns to make a couple of back payments to Household Finance, and had to borrow one from our host.

During breakfast I noticed a couple of fat old beagle hounds, farting and wheezing, their noses stuck as far into the fireplace as they could get without burning themselves, snoozing happily in the warmth. Their names, I learned, were Rocket and Queenie, though I figured it was at least 10 years since Rocket earned that handle.

When we were ready to go shoot some rabbits, John says to the pooches, "Vut mine doggies like to go huntin' mit mine frrrriends?"

They struggle to an upright position, yawn, fart, and waddle down the porch steps and into the car, panting, either from the excitement of the hunt, or exhaustion, I'm not sure which.

Conway and Jim drop John and me off at one end of a big stand of hardwoods, and take the dogs with them to the other end, maybe a half-mile away. Pretty soon we hear the dogs yo-yo-yoing, like they do, and I give the borrowed 12 gauge double a couple of practice swings, and check the safety. John suggests we spread out a little. Before we do, he claps one hand on my shoulder, looks me dead in the eye and says, "Shimmy, I don't know how much rrrabbit-huntin you haff done, but ven zer dogs is bugling, und your heart iss pounding - ker-thunk, ker-thunk in your shest, und you got zer gun oop, rrremember vun ting; rrrabbits got ears vot point oop, und mine doggies got ears vot point down!"

And he walked off, leaving me a little awed by the simple directness of his point, and remembering that more than one good rabbit dog had died of lead shot in his liver, put there by an over-anxious shooter.

John has long-since gone to that great hunting lodge in the sky, but every time I go rabbit hunting, I think fondly of him and his "doggies," and wish him auf Wiedersehen.

GRAVY, IT CAN MAKE OR BREAK YOU

Gravy, to be poured generously, piping hot, over your deer roast and the mashed potatoes, to be sopped up with hunks of soft French bread, poured over homemade biscuits, or to reheat leftovers in, can be the making of a meal. Leave it out and something fine is missing. Make it badly—full of grease, lumpy with flour, or thin and watery—and you have screwed up what might have been a wonderful meal.

Perhaps nowhere in the cooking process is your own individual sense of taste as critical as here...to know when it needs a pinch of something else, or (perhaps even more importantly) when to leave it alone...to quit while you're ahead.

In the *Stews, Soups and Chowders* section, you'll find instructions for making stock; for meat, fish, or birds. If you have prepared stock in advance, you're a leg up in gravy making. If not, you can still make an excellent gravy from scratch without much trouble.

BASIC BIRD GRAVY

2 cups stock *or*
2 cups water and two chicken bouillon cubes
1 medium onion, quartered
1 carrot, peeled, cut in 3 or 4 pieces
1 stalk celery, cut in 3 or 4 pieces, including leaves
1 pinch thyme
1 pinch sage (optional)
1/3 cup white wine
neck, giblets, heart, liver, and a small piece of body fat from the bird or birds you're cooking
pepper and salt to taste (bouillon cubes are already salty, so be careful)

Put all ingredients into a sauce pan, bring to a boil, reduce heat, cover, and simmer for one hour, stirring occasionally. Remove cover after one hour, raise the heat a little and cook uncovered for another half hour to reduce. Strain through a strainer or colander. Return liquid to pan and set aside until roast is done. Then add four or five tablespoons of pan drippings and thicken with a package of turkey gravy mix, *or* two tablespoons flour *or* corn starch mixed into a paste with a couple of jiggers of cold water. In either case, raise the heat under the gravy and stir constantly while thickening. Pour into a preheated bowl or gravy boat and serve piping hot.

Note: When adding pan drippings, take as little grease as possible. Pour off most of the pan grease into a coffee or beer can, and get to the juices and stuff stuck to the bottom of the pan. If the gravy gets too greasy in spite of your best efforts, pour it into a jar or bowl and set it in the refrigerator, or out in the snow, while you are carving the birds, and serving dinner. By that time the fat will have risen to the top and begun to congeal. Pour it off, reheat and restir and you're all set.

If the gravy gets lumpy while thickening, pour through a strainer, reheat, and use.

What about the neck and innards you used to begin with? I usually whack the necks into pieces about an inch long, cut the livers, giblets and hearts in half, and put them, along with the vegetables on a plate with a little pepper and salt, and let the guys pick on it while they're having a drink. *Or*, pick most of the meat off the necks, chop it up fine along with the giblets, livers and hearts, and add back into the gravy. *Or*, throw it out.

BASIC MEAT GRAVY

2 cups of stock *or*
2 cups water and 2 beef bouillon cubes *or*
1 can beef bouillon plus water to equal 2 cups
1 medium onion, cut in quarters
1 stalk celery, cut in 3 or 4 pieces, including leaves
1 carrot, cut in 3 or 4 pieces
1 bay leaf
1 pinch thyme
1 pinch basil
1 clove garlic, whole or finely minced
1/3 cup red wine
a bone from the roast, if you have it

As with the bird gravy, put all ingredients into a sauce pan, bring to a boil, reduce heat to simmer, cover and cook slowly for one hour, stirring occasionally. Remove lid and cook another half hour to reduce. Strain. Add pan juices, thicken with one package brown or mushroom gravy mix, *or* 2 tablespoons flour *or* corn starch mixed into a paste over medium-high heat until thickened. Strain again if necessary.

Note: Don't over salt. Bouillon, either canned or in cubes is already salty. Reducing the liquid tends to make it saltier still. Taste it frequently and add salt sparingly. If you think you will need more than two cups of gravy, increase all ingredients proportionately.

Gravy should complement the meat it is served with, not fight it. These two recipes are *basic*. By all means change them to fit the ingredients called for in the roast recipe they are to accompany.

For instance, if the basic recipe calls for juniper berries and 2 oz. of Cognac, add a few crushed juniper berries to the gravy mix, and substitute Cognac for the red wine. Or if your duck or pheasant recipe calls for orange slices and white wine, add a little orange juice to the water, or orange slices, and substitute Grand Marnier or Triple Sec for the white wine.

Be creative with gravy. Experiment, try different things. The worst that can happen is that you screw it up so badly that it tastes terrible. In which case, don't serve it. Throw it out, whip out another package of gravy mix, follow the directions and serve. Live to fight another day.

And try not to dribble it all over your good hunting shirt.

PREPARING THE MEAT

Every hunter I've ever known has his own theory about what to do with a deer after he's shot it. The only thing they all agree on is that it should be gutted, or field-dressed, as thoroughly and quickly as possible, and cooled out. After that, it seems to be every man for himself.

Do you hang it for a couple of days or a couple of weeks, or not at all? Do you skin it right away, or later? Do you wash the meat in vinegar? Soak it for 24 hours? Cut the haunches into various roasts, or just cut them in half, or cook them whole. Do you bleed the dear by cutting it's throat? Do you remove all the bones from roasts, or leave them in? The answer to all these questions is *yes* except when it's *no*.

Let's start with the field dressing. If the animal has been gut-shot, or I've made a mess of dressing it out, I'll wash out the cavity with a mild solution of vinegar and water when I get it back to camp and hung up. Otherwise, plain water or snow will do. If you soak the animal with vinegar, he's going to *taste* like vinegar.

Just make sure you gut it clean...no esophagus, urine, pellets or anything else left in there that will eventually stink and make the meat taste bad.

Hanging? I've done it both ways. It depends on the weather, whether I got lucky and got my deer on the first day of a six day trip, or got him on the last day, and whether I'm going to play Nanook of the North and do the whole thing myself, or turn the entire operation over to my friends at the local meat-locker.

For instance; you are sitting in a tree stand on the very first day of the season, early in the rut. A good looking 8-point buck wanders by, totally unaware of your deadly presence. You aim carefully and squeeze off a round from the old thutty-thutty, BLAMMO!

He goes down like he was pole-axed and twitches nary a twitch. That's going to be a tender deer, friend. He was relaxed, hadn't yet lost what little body fat he had by screwing his brains out, fighting with all the other bucks, and generally running around like crazy. You don't need to "tenderize " him by hanging. Gut him, drag him back to camp, skin him and butcher him. Have some for dinner that night.

Later in the rut, a deer that you've managed to gut-shoot, or otherwise mis-hit, or one that is running hell-for-leather, is going to be all full of adrenaline, his every fiber tight and stiff, and may well benefit from hanging in the cool air for a few days. I find it easier to skin a deer when the body is still warm and the hide supple. Your call.

I don't believe in bleeding a deer or elk. They have so little body fat that the blood is all they have to make the meat juicy and flavorful. I neither bleed them nor soak the meat to draw the blood out. Soaking tends to make the meat mushy, particularly if you are going to freeze it. Don't.

I generally leave most of the bones in, convinced that the bones add flavor; but am pretty scrupulous about cutting out every last bit of fat. Deer fat, what little there is, gets rancid pretty quickly, both before and after cooking. Like sin, it should be cast out! As should as much membrane and tallow as you have the patience for.

I'm not a skilled-enough butcher to take apart the haunches into their individual components...eye, bottom and top round, loin, rump, etc. Every time I've tried it I've bitched it up. If you know how, by all means, go to it and blessings on thee. I usually cut the haunch in halves, giving me a butt end and a shank end, like two halves of a ham. And like ham, I cut a thick steak off each side of that center cut. I also cut the hocks off the bottom of the shank end. They are great in stew or bean and barley soup.

So, from the rear legs I end up with two hocks, four ham steaks, and four roasts, suitable for either dry oven roasting or pot roasting. Following the same procedure, generally, on the front legs, you'll get four medium-sized pot roasts.

I like the tenderloin, so peel the back straps out whole. If you prefer chops, cut across the spine; but there goes your filet mignon. Again, your call.

I usually get two or three small roasts from the neck. It's delicious meat. Just remember to peel, pull, or cut out the tendons. They are tough and bad-tasting. If you prefer, the neck meat, along with the brisket and whatever else you have left can be ground up for hamburger, or cubed for stew or chili.

On a big enough animal, the ribs are good for barbecue.

Which leaves us the innards. I happen to love the heart, liver and kidneys, and have enjoyed them all in a variety of ways. There are those who cannot abide even the thought of eating organ meats. It's your deer; do what you want with them. If you are going to use the organs, be sure to cut away *all the fat* in and around them.

In reading over the above paragraphs, I seem to have assumed that this particular deer died of a stroke, or maybe that we scared him to death; for nowhere have I discussed bullet damage. Just remember to cut out badly damaged meat and all the congealed blood that accumulates along the bullet path and final destination.

Now, wash each piece of meat thoroughly, getting rid of all hair, sludge, gunk and what have you, and pat dry with paper towels or whatever is handy; but do dry it.

Wrap each piece at least twice; better yet, three times. Twice in freezer paper, sealing tightly with masking tape, and making sure no jagged bone ends are going to cut through the paper.

Using a magic marker, mark each piece with the cut and date, then place in one of those large plastic, zip-lock bags, squeezing all the air out as you zip its zipper. Properly wrapped, your cache of deer meat should last in the freezer from 6 months to a year.

If you're going to grind meat for hamburger, use an old-fashioned meat grinder like your grandmother had. You can still get them through the Sears catalogue, restaurant supply outlets and specialty stores. If you prefer the look and feel of mushy paste, use a modern food processor.

Wrap your ground or cubed meat in one pound packages the same way you wrapped the larger roasts, identifying and dating the packages prior to freezing.

A word about tools. If all you have is your old Buck knife, or the trusty K-Bar your Dad carried at Guadalcanal, so be it. But the job is a hell of a lot easier if you have a decent ax, a meat saw, a good-sized butcher knife, a smaller boning or paring knife, a sharpening stone or steel, and lots of clean rags. The layer of waxy tallow that keeps the deer warm in place of body fat, collects on knife blades, and quickly dulls them. Wipe your blades clean and resharpen them frequently.

Cleanly killed, quickly and efficiently field-dressed and cooled down, properly butchered, cleaned and freezer-wrapped, your deer meat is ready for the pan or oven. Assuming you follow the recipes carefully, the meat will be tender, flavorful, and juicy.

Should one of your dinner guests later claim it was "tough," or worse yet, "gamy," resist the temptation to brain him or her with an iron skillet. Just don't invite him back...ever! There's not much future in casting pearls before swine.

It's possible that you will disagree with some or *all* of what I have said in this chapter. Feel free to do it your own way. I've written what has worked best for me over the years, and I'm satisfied to let it go at that.

EQUIPMENT

Years ago a bunch of us hunted out of a cabin on the shore of Horseshoe Lake, just below Tupper Lake, in the Adirondack Mountains of New York State. The cabin was a line shack for the old New York Central Railroad on a spur that ran from Herkimer to Lake Placid, and came equipped with the biggest damned coal-burning stove I ever saw.

Our host, Al Rocsen, who leased the cabin from the Central, claimed the stove came out of an old caboose. All I know for sure was that the cast iron monster had room for everything—six big burners, removable lids that let the heat really get to your pots and pans, two bake ovens, a keep-warm oven, and a kind of ledge on the back of the stove where there was just enough heat to keep your chili or bean soup pot bubbly hot all day. Besides cooking on it, we heated the cabin with it as well. It ate hundred pound bags of pea-coal like a kid eating Snickers.

Once I learned how to use the dampers, and to regulate the heat in that rascal, it was the most marvelous cooking machine that ever was, and cooking for 6, 8, or 10 hunters was a real piece of cake. Al had every pot, pan, skillet and utensil known to man, and though we didn't take as many deer as we wanted, we ate like kings.

Death, retirement and divorce took their toll on that group. I went back to hunt there some years later with a cousin of mine. The key was no longer under the linoleum in the outhouse, and the place was all boarded up. We pitched a tent on the lee side of the cabin to protect us from the bitter, snow-laden winds that blew across the lake, and did our cooking on a two-burner Coleman stove and a roaring campfire. We hunted well and ate well, but I kept thinking of that great iron monster inside the cabin, cold and unused while we busted our chops and froze right outside the door.

The point is, I guess, that as far as stoves go, you must make the best of what's available. If you're going to hunt out of the back of a pickup truck and cook on a two-burner propane stove, make sure you bring a sturdy grill for the campfire. It will hold your coffee pot, skillet, or Dutch oven; will grill your steaks, boil clean-up water and provide a good bit of psychological warmth.

Of necessity, you'll be limited in the number of pots and pans you can use efficiently. If you have your own cabin, or have regular access to one, you can accumulate all manner of equipment and accessories.

As a bare minimum I would have the following:

1 10-12" cast iron skillet
1 10-12" teflon-coated skillet
1 12-cup coffee pot
3 sauce pans of different capacities
1 cast iron Dutch oven, 8-quart, with lid
1 large pot for boiling spaghetti water, etc.
1 colander or strainer
1 spatula for flipping hotcakes, eggs, etc.
1 large spoon, plain
1 large spoon, slotted
1 large meat fork
1 griddle, flat
1 good carving knife
1 good paring or boning knife
A couple of wooden spoons for stirring stews and soups, mixing pancake batter, scrambled eggs, etc.

The cast iron skillet is great for frying potatoes, sautéing onions, braising meat, etc. I usually keep the teflon-coated one for frying or scrambling eggs or anything else where sticking is a problem.

Your sauce pans are for boiling eggs, making gravy, cooking veggies, boiling potatoes, etc. and should be big enough to handle the job. Covers or lids help. The lid to my big spaghetti pot fits my fry pans, and that's a help.

For me the indispensable item is the Dutch oven. This versatile beauty can be used on a modern gas or electric stove or oven, on a propane stove, or on a grill over a campfire. In it you can make stew, soup, chili, or spaghetti sauce. You can braise or pot roast in it. You can even bake a cake in it. I wouldn't be without at least one of them, in camp or at home.

With these items you ought to be able to cope with most any cooking situation that comes up, whether you're in a tent, a hunting lodge, or your own home. Such niceties as poultry shears, lemon juicers and a hundred other gadgets can be acquired as you perceive the need for them, and can be toted along or left behind as seems appropriate.

The important thing is to know what kind of meals you'll be cooking in what kind of environment; then bring the tools you'll need.

...I still think that one of the pleasantest of all emotions
is to know that I,
I with my brain and my hands, have nourished my beloved few,
that I have concocted a stew or a story,
a rarity or a plain dish,
to sustain them truly against the hungers of the world.

M.F.K. Fisher
The Art of Eating

ON BEING CAMP COOK,
or:
HOW DID I LET MYSELF GET TALKED INTO THIS IN THE FIRST PLACE?

The four hunters arrived in camp, began to unpack and get settled in. When the subject of cooking came up, no one volunteered, so they drew straws. The loser was to cook until somebody complained, then the complainer took over.

Obviously, the guy who drew the short straw was none too happy, and over the next couple of days turned out some pretty bad meals; the bacon undercooked, the eggs overcooked, the toast burned, the pork chops heavy with grease. There was some grumbling, but no one complained.

Desperate to get out of the hated chore, he detoured through a farm field on the way back to camp one evening, and there collected a couple of pounds of horse manure. Back at camp before his buddies got there, he mixed the road apples with onions, egg and spices, and baked a "meat loaf."

The rest of the party arrived, ravenous, as usual, and after a few drinks and lots of good cheer, sat to table, feasting their eyes on a piping hot meat loaf, steaming gravy, bowls of mashed potatoes and vegetables, and a bottle of red wine. After a cheer for the cook, they dug in lustily.

After the first couple of bites, the room grew silent, the men toying with their food, none daring to look the cook in the eye. Finally, one threw down his fork in disgust, and exclaimed,"Gawddamn! This tastes like horse #@%$&#...but GOOD, but GOOD!"

Sometimes that's the way it is; but it doesn't have to be, and by all means choosing the cook should be taken care of long before arriving in camp.

Assuming that *you* are going to be camp cook, it follows that you will also do the meal-planning and shopping. Suppose there are six of you, and you'll be in camp six days..that's 108 meals; 36 breakfasts, 36 lunches, and 36 dinners! Frightening? Not to worry; with a little planning, it'll be a breeze.

MEAL PLANNING

How you hunt will determine how and when you eat. If you are all young and eager, leave camp at 5 a.m. and don't come back 'til dark, plan on just juice, coffee, tea, milk and donuts at 5:15, and pack sturdy bag lunches, with meat and cheese sandwiches, also peanut butter and jelly, some cookies, a couple of candy bars and a piece of fruit. Then you really only have to worry about one big meal at night.

In a lot of camps I've been in, a variation of that is what usually happens. Get up at 5, dress, gobble a donut and a cup of coffee, and maybe a glass of juice, pack a modest lunch of a sandwich, candy bar and piece of fruit (to be eaten around 9 or 10 o'clock), then wander back to camp around 11:30 or 12, sitting down then to a hearty brunch, which may include a Bloody Mary or two, or a screwdriver, just to clear the dust of the trail from our throats, then a nap, and swapping of theories on where the damn deer have gone to. Back to the woods around 2:30 or 3, hunt until dark, back in for cocktails and dinner around 7 p.m.

Of course, if you're old and out of shape (like me and my editor and long-time hunting buddy, Don Steffen), you let the young studs stumble around in the dark. You sleep in 'til a reasonable hour, eat a little breakfast and, knowing from pre-opening day scouting, that a prime buck is apt to inspect a particular scrape around 10 or so, wander over there in time to dispatch him with a minimum of fuss and feathers.

In any case, talk it over with the other hunters in your party, lay out a meal schedule, and stick to it. Plan the menu for the week and fly it by them. Don't wait 'til you get to camp to discover that one of the guys can't eat pork chops, and another will eat only peanut butter and India relish sandwiches for lunch.

A week's menu might look like this:

Breakfast

Every day: juice, cold cereal, milk, coffee and fruit, plus:

Sat.   Bacon, eggs, toast.
Sun.   Sausage, pancakes, toast.
Mon.   Oatmeal, English muffins
Tue.   Ham, eggs, biscuits.
Wed.   Bacon, eggs, toast.
Thu.   Sausage, fried mush, English muffins.

Lunch

Hot chili or soup, assorted cheeses and luncheon meats for sandwiches, pickles and relishes, coffee, tea, milk, beer, pop, cookies, candy bars.

Dinner

Sat.   Grilled sirloin steaks with Chef's butter, baked potatoes, lima beans, salad, bread, butter, pears Belle Helène.

Sun.   Chicken Marengo, cottage-fried potatoes, campfire corn, salad, pound cake à la mode.

Mon.   Pot roast of beef with carrots, potatoes, onions and mushrooms, bread, butter, canned peach halves.

Tue.   Bean and barley soup, baked pork chops with sauerkraut, potatoes and onions, bread, butter, salad, cold fruit cocktail with ice cream.

Wed.   Dips and chips, tacos with chili, sour cream, onions, cheese, refried beans, cold fruit de jour.

Thu.   Italian spaghetti with meatballs salad, hot garlic bread, mixed fresh fruit and melon.

Throughout the week: crackers and cheese, dips and chips, etc. for cocktail hour; cookies, candy bars and other munchies.

This menu assumes that you get skunked in the deer department, which is sometimes a fair assumption, and must fill yourselves on store-bought meals. It also assumes six men with healthy appetites, made even healthier by being out in the woods all day, which is to say that they'll eat like animals. O.K., here's how you shop. Break it up into categories.

SHOPPING

Meat & Deli

3 lbs. sausage links, 3 lbs. bacon, 3 large ham steaks, 1 ½ lbs. each, sliced boiled ham, roast beef, bologna, turkey breast, corned beef, American cheese and Swiss cheese, 2 lbs. cubed round steak, 1 lb. cubed lean pork, 2 packages smoked ham hocks, 6 10 - 12 oz. boneless sirloin steaks, rib eyes or T-bones, 18 chicken thighs, 7 - 9 lb. pot roast (top or bottom round, rump, loin, etc.), 12 thick pork chops, 2 lbs. ground round (for meatballs), 1 lb. each sweet and hot Italian sausage, cheese for munchies (5 lbs. assorted cheddar, bleu, brie—your call).

Fruits & Vegetables

6 grapefruit, 1 large bunch bananas, 4 boxes berries, 4 large tart green apples, 2 or 3 lbs. apples, 3 lbs. grapes, 6 pears, 2 lemons, 15 lbs. new potatoes, 6 large baking potatoes, 10 lbs. onions, 2 lbs. carrots, 2 lbs. fresh mushrooms, 3 heads lettuce, 2 heads romaine, 1 doz. tomatoes, 2 bunches scallions, 2 large red onions, 2 heads garlic, 6 jalapeño or chile peppers.

Dairy

2 gallons fruit juice, 3 ½ doz. extra-large eggs, 1 lb. butter, 2 lbs. margarine, 1 gallon milk, 2 pints sour cream, 1 large container Parmesan or Romano cheese, 2 lb. package grated sharp cheddar cheese.

Canned Goods

1 large box Bisquick, 1 quart maple syrup, 1 box Quaker Oats, 1 jar grape jelly, 2 large variety packs cold cereal, 1 large jar peanut butter, mustard, mayo, catsup, 1 package Wick Fowler's 2-Alarm chili, 2 cans chili beans, 5 large cans Italian plum tomatoes, 2 cans refried beans, 3 jars salsa, 1 can tomato paste, 1 lb. dried split peas, navy beans or lentils—your choice, 1 lb. bag barley, 2 large cans each, pears, peaches, fruit cocktail, 2 or 3 bottles prepared salad dressing, 1 bottle cooking/salad oil, 1 bottle olive oil, 1 bottle wine vinegar, 1 jar each sweet/sour/dill pickles, stuffed olives, relish, 1 can condensed milk, 3 lbs. coffee, 1 bottle steak sauce, 1 bottle Worcestershire sauce, Tabasco sauce, 1 small bottle molasses, 2 lbs. spaghetti noodles, 2 cans sauerkraut, 1 small jar caraway seeds, 1 lb. flour, 1 lb. bag cornmeal, 1 can chocolate syrup, 2 dozen taco shells, 1 small can bread crumbs, 1 lb. sugar, tea bags, spices (see spice section on page 16).

Bakery
3 large loaves white bread, 4 loaves rye bread, 2 packages English muffins, 2 boxes donuts, 2 boxes sticky buns or sweet rolls.

Frozen Foods
3 containers guacamole, 2 large packages frozen mixed vegetables (Italian, Bavarian, Oriental), campfire corn, lima beans, 2 frozen pound cakes, 3 loaves garlic bread, 1 gallon ice cream. (If you have a freezer in camp, buy it at the last outpost of civilization before heading into the woods.)

Munchies
2 large bags of small candy bars, 4 boxes cookies, 6 boxes assorted crackers, 6 bags assorted chips, 6 containers of dip.

Paper Products
Paper bags (for packing lunches), paper napkins, paper towels, plastic coated paper plates, zip-lock sandwich bags, large zip-lock food storage bags, plastic wrap, aluminum foil, dish washing liquid, kitchen sponge, pot scrubber, toilet paper and 2 bars hand soap.

Obviously, you can omit some items and add others, but what I've listed will cover you for the menu we laid out. Keep the cash register check, divide it by six, and be sure to collect.

I have three large Coleman coolers. I usually buy three bags of ice cubes and three blocks of ice, put a block in each cooler, pack the perishables (milk, eggs, meat, butter, etc.) in them, add beer and soda, and pack cubes on top. If your camp has a freezer and refrigerator, fine; otherwise the food will keep in the coolers just as well, as long as you replenish the ice as necessary.

If the guys want you to, buy beer and soda pop for them and add it to the tab. Two cases of beer (if you can agree on a brand), and two of assorted pop, should do nicely for openers. The same with wine; a large jug each of red and white (See wine section, page 14) will do, and add it to the bill. Let each member of the party supply his own drinkin' likker.

O.K., we've planned our menu, and bought what we need; what now?

COOKING

For one thing, you can make a big pot of chili, and one of bean soup, and your spaghetti sauce with meatballs and sausage, at home. Freeze them in tupperware tubs and bring them to camp, thaw, heat and eat. This is a big time saver. For another, several of the dinners are one pot meals that cook slowly for two or three hours on low heat (pot roast, spaghetti and meatballs, chili). The pork chops with apples, onions, potatoes and sauerkraut, also are cooked together in your Dutch oven or a big roasting pan covered and sealed with aluminum foil. Put these items on low heat before you go out for the afternoon hunt.

Perhaps most importantly, you elect, appoint, short-straw, or otherwise "volunteer" yourself a #2—an assistant cook. He sets the table, helps with peeling onions and potatoes, washing and cutting up salad greens, firing up the stove in the morning, putting the coffee on, general food prep and serving.

Neither of you do any KP, cleaning up, chopping firewood or any other general camp chores whatever. Let the other guys understand up front what the division of labor is. You want the kitchen cleaned up after each meal, so you can start the next one with clean pots, pans, dishes and utensils. If they dope off on you and you come in a little early one night to start dinner, only to find the kitchen a shambles of dirty dishes and greasy pots, make yourself a drink, go sit by the fire and rest your bones. When they get in, hungry as wolves, and find you a bustle of absolutely no activity whatever, they'll turn to in a hurry, and I guarantee you it won't happen again.

Read over your recipes; know what kind and how much preparation is involved, and what chores you can relegate to your #2, maintaining your own responsibility for the main course.

I use new potatoes, particularly small, red ones. They need only be washed and sliced and don't require peeling. In fact, cut up and boiled in their jackets, they are delicious with just butter and salt. But boiled, fried or included in stew or pot roasts, don't bother to peel them.

Have #2 take care of the salad at night. Use the regular lettuce except for Caesar salad where you use romaine. Have him wash and drain the leaves, breaking them up into fork-sized pieces. Put them in a large bowl, chop up a bit of red onion or scallion, add a couple of tomatoes cut in quarters or eighths, sprinkle a bit of parsley or sweet basil on it and serve. Let the hunters add their own dressing from the bottled ones you bought.

You make the Caesar salad Thursday night, serving it before the spaghetti and meatballs. Separate all the leaves from the head. Wash and dry them. Break them into fork-sized pieces, discarding the outside leaves, using the crispier parts nearer the center.

Pour about two ounces of olive oil or light cooking oil into your salad bowl, add a dash or two of Worcestershire sauce, a squeeze of lemon juice, a clove or two of finely minced garlic, a scant teaspoon of mustard, and a pinch of basil. Smush this all around in the bottom of the bowl with the back of a spoon. Toss your romaine leaves in this, sprinkle on grated Italian cheese, salt, fresh cracked pepper, and croutons, if you have them. Toss again and serve.

I've left out the anchovies, which many people don't like, and the almost raw egg, which I now hear is not such a healthy thing to eat; so strictly speaking, it's not a real Caesar salad. But it's good and Italiany, and will be a great starter for your spaghetti and meatballs.

Saturday night's dinner menu calls for Chef's Butter to put on the broiled steaks. Gary Barrone, chef and co-owner of Gary's Restaurant in Washington, DC, gave me this quick and easy recipe:

Chef's Butter

Let a stick of butter come to room temperature in a small bowl. When it's "workable" add a clove of minced garlic, 5 or 6 crushed green peppercorns, a scant pinch of thyme, and a pinch of rosemary, basil or oregano, crushed up as fine as you can make it. Add a half ounce of bourbon if you like. Blend thoroughly and refrigerate for an hour or two.

All the dinner recipes are found in the appropriate sections of this book. Prep time should be no more than half an hour on any of them, and cooking time varies from half an hour to three hours depending on the meal, the stove, and the altitude. Don't ask me why, but things take longer to cook over 5,000 ft. At 10,000 ft. a boiled egg that usually takes 3 minutes, can take 6. Experiment a little. Baked potatoes take longer, too; up to an hour and a half for a good sized one.

If your camp has an oven, make sure #2 puts it on low as soon as he gets up in the morning and into camp in the afternoon. Use it to warm plates to keep hot meals hot, to keep buttered toast, biscuits, muffins and bacon, ham or sausage hot after they've been cooked, while you're cooking eggs or hot cereal, or steaks.

Unless you're a masochist, don't get involved cooking eggs to order, sunnyside up, over easy, or whatever. Scramble them, beating them in a bowl with a little milk, pouring them into buttered, heated pans (medium heat) and stirring constantly with a wooden spoon until done. Spoon into a heated bowl and serve immediately. Bacon, ham and sausages should be cooked first, drained, and kept warm in the oven. You can broil the ham steaks or fry them in a little water. Cut them in half and serve them hot.

There's a great recipe for drop biscuits on the Bisquick box. They're easy to make, and a nice change from toast. If you don't have a cookie sheet, your griddle will do in a pinch. An excellent pancake recipe is also printed on the Bisquick box.

If you have some left over pot roast and a couple of potatoes from dinner, try this at breakfast next day. Chop up a fresh onion, the meat, and the potatoes, and fry in a little butter, stirring it together, just 'til everything gets heated through. Then fold in your scrambled egg mixture, keep stirring, and cook 'til the eggs are done. It's a winner.

Hot cereal—oatmeal or corn meal mush—are a nice change from eggs, and provide a hearty, nourishing breakfast. Serve it hot with butter, milk, sugar and cinnamon. Make twice as much corn meal mush as you think you'll need. Pour the leftover mush into a bread pan and refrigerate for a day or so. Then slice and fry it for breakfast, covered with hot syrup, and served with bacon or sausage.

Keep the small individual boxes of cold cereal on the table at breakfast, along with some bananas and some berries, which your #2 has washed and picked clean. Some guys will have them instead of or along with whatever else you're serving. They also make good snacks.

You'll notice in this section and throughout the book, I don't fuss much with desserts for after dinner. A slice of pound cake, cold canned fruit, or a big scoop of ice cream will usually do very well. If one of the guys feels like whipping up a batch of brownies or an apple pie, by all means let him be your guest. Better yet, have him make them in advance and bring them along.

I cheat on the pears *Belle Helène*, which are wonderful, but too fussy for camp. Put two pear halves on a slice of pound cake. Put a small scoop of vanilla ice cream in the center of each half, and pour warm chocolate syrup over the top. Voila! Nine million calories, but what the hell.

Remember that most guys eat like they have two backsides when in camp. Have plenty of fruit, candy bars, granola bars, chips, doodles and munchies of all kinds.

That's really all there is to it. With a little planning, cooking and freezing some things in advance, and doing a couple of one-pot meals (and with a lot of help from your #2), you can be camp cook, serving good, hearty meals without being a slave to the stove, and still enjoy the hunt to the fullest.

You get something else out of it, too. You get that sense of pride that comes from knowing *you* did it. With your own mind, your own heart and your own hands, you nourished your favored companions. It's a good feeling.

A last thought. You and your helper work hard to get hot meals cooked and served. Meals are ready when *you* say they're ready, not 10 minutes later when some guy stumbles out of the sack, scratching his backside. You are the Lord of the Kitchen. Be firm.

A recipe is supposed to be a formula,
a means prescribed for producing a desired result,
whether that be an atomic weapon,
a well-trained Pekingese,
or an omelet.

M.F.K. Fisher
With Bold Knife & Fork

BIG GAME

The love affair that develops between the hunter and his quarry is hard to explain to non-hunters. I gave up trying long ago. But it certainly exists, particularly with big game; whether it's with white tail or mule deer, elk, bear, wild boar, moose, antelope, big horned sheep, or mountain goats. These are the kings of the forest, swamps, and mountains. We hunt them because we are hunters and because we must, just as others climb mountains "because they are there."

We work hard at it, frequently coming up empty. Some of us spend tubs of money doing it; air travel, pack-mules, guides and the rest. When we *are* successful, we feel our efforts are justified and we are at peace, with ourselves and the game we have brought home.

Now, in feeding us, these beautiful animals have fulfilled their destiny. Because we value them so highly, they deserve our best efforts in preparing and cooking them. What follows are some of the best recipes I have come across in three decades. I hope you enjoy them.

Many of them are interchangeable; deer for elk, elk for moose, all three for beef.

Bon appétit!

VENISON TENDERLOIN ANTRIM

Doug Bury, long-time owner of the Antrim Lodge in the Catskill Mountain town of Roscoe, NY, served venison tenderloin (back strap) to favored guests. It was the best I have ever tasted.

1 or 2 deer tenderloins
¼ lb. butter
3 or 4 garlic cloves, minced
1 or 2 oz. red wine
1 or 2 oz. bourbon
2 tbsp. currant jelly
ground black pepper
toast points

Toast at least a half-dozen slices of white or rye bread, cut in half diagonally and arrange around the outside edge of a meat platter, place in a 250 degree oven.

Peel or cut away any fat or membrane from the tenderloin. You should have a piece of meat 18 inches long, roughly triangular at the heavy end, tapering off nearly flat at the other. Slice it across the grain in pieces ½ inch thick. Pepper them liberally, do not salt. Set aside. Mince garlic and set aside.

Melt butter in a large, well-seasoned cast iron skillet over a high flame. When the butter is crackling, spitting, and smoking, sprinkle in the garlic and add the meat, searing each piece for about ½ minute on each side, no more. You want it slightly blackened on the outside, rare and juicy on the inside. Put them on the hot platter and back in the oven.

Reduce the heat under the skillet, add the wine, bourbon, and currant jelly, smushing it around a little bit, mixing it well with the burnt butter and any bits of meat stuck to the pan. Pour over the venison and serve immediately.

A staunch burgundy or cold dark beer goes well with this, as do boiled mashed turnips, red cabbage, or buttered egg noodles.

For variations, substitute Cognac or Grand Marnier for the bourbon, add 5 or 6 crushed juniper berries and/or green peppercorns to the minced garlic, or substitute loin chops for the meat, cooking them about 1½ to 2 minutes a side, depending on how thick they are.

BUCK HAVEN VENISON DINNER

Jack Lamson, owner of the Buck Haven Deer Camp near Burlington, VT, sent me the following recipe for a full dinner featuring venison steaks or chops, spiced simply, and served hot and rare.

venison chops or steaks
unflavored meat tenderizer
Worcestershire sauce
garlic salt
Mrs. Dash's original seasoning
sautéed fresh mushrooms and onions

Bring venison to room temperature. Lay out on a cutting board, remove all fat, and pierce with a large fork over the entire surface, on both sides. For less tender cuts, such as round steak, sprinkle with unflavored meat tenderizer. This is not necessary for chops or other choice cuts. Using your fingers, spread a limited amount of Worcestershire sauce over the entire surface of both sides of the meat. Add a few shakes of garlic salt and a little of the Mrs. Dash's. Cover the meat with plastic wrap and let it stand for 30 - 40 minutes.

When the rest of the meal is nearly ready, sauté the onions and mushrooms in some butter or light oil in an iron skillet. When done, remove and set aside. Cook the steaks or chops in the same skillet at medium-high heat, until done medium rare to rare. The onions and mushrooms can be served as a side dish, or poured over the meat. Be sure to serve it *hot*. Jack says: "We like to complete the meal with hand mashed potatoes with diced onions and a hunter gravy made from Knorr's Hunter Sauce Mix (we add some of the mushrooms and onions to it) and a veggie of choice. A bottle or two of Merlot is a great complement to this meal."

To which I can only add, try a 1987 M.G. Vallejo Merlot from the Glen Ellen vineyards in California. Though modestly priced, it's full-bodied, rich and soft on the throat.

SKEWERED VENISON WITH BOURBON

2 lbs. cubed deer meat or elk
1 cup cooking oil
½ cup red wine
½ cup bourbon
pinch each, thyme, basil, oregano
½ tsp. cracked pepper
½ tsp. salt
1 or 2 garlic cloves, minced or crushed
Fresh cherry tomatoes, whole fresh mushrooms, cut-up green peppers, quartered onions.

Place all ingredients in a large bowl, mix thoroughly and set aside for 5 or 6 hours.

Place the venison on skewers, alternating with the vegetables. Cook on an open fire or grill until done medium rare.

You can vary this shish kebab by adding hot peppers to the marinade, and any other veggies you like. Serve with homemade potato salad or cole slaw, French bread and red wine, it makes a fine supper.

A WORD ABOUT LARDING...

Many of the recipes that follow, particularly those that call for a dry oven roasting method, also call for larding...adding fat to the meat internally. I've never learned how to handle a larding needle effectively and, instead, I poke holes in the meat, stuffing them with bacon, salt pork, lard, margarine, or butter, and sometimes mixing a little spice with the larding ingredient.

The pointed end of a knife-sharpening steel or a decent-sized Phillips screwdriver make great larding holes, easy to stuff with whatever ingredient you choose.

ROAST VENISON IN A BAG

1 shoulder of venison
1 can golden mushroom soup, or onion soup
1 cup red wine
1 garlic clove, minced
1 package brown gravy mix
10 juniper berries, crushed
salt and cracked pepper to taste

Wipe roast dry and lard it in 5 or 6 places. Place in plastic oven bag. Mix other ingredients and pour over roast inside the bag. Seal the bag, cut one or two slits in the top, and place in an oven roasting pan. Roast in 350 degree oven 2½ to 3 hours.

When the roast is done, remove from bag and place on a hot platter. Let it stand for a few minutes while you strain the gravy and reheat it till it's bubbling.

Since you'll have plenty of rich gravy, mashed potatoes or boiled quartered new potatoes in their skins are a good choice, along with a green vegetable and salad.

ROAST HAUNCH OF VENISON STUART

Back in 1982, The Country Publishers brought out a fine game cookbook written by Charles E. Stuart. Some of Stuart's recipes were absolutely dynamite. This is one of them, and I suspect it would be equally good using elk or moose.

1 10 lb. hind quarter
¼ lb. butter
3 strips bacon
3 juniper berries
1 tbsp. salt
4 cups hearty red wine
1 medium onion, quartered
1 pinch paprika
½ tbsp. cracked pepper

This recipe takes two days. The first night, marinate the haunch in wine, turning frequently. The following day take the haunch and make three deep holes evenly spaced along the meat. Plug these with a strip of raw bacon and quarter onion. Over this sprinkle salt, pepper and paprika. Place the meat back in the marinade, add the juniper berries and refrigerate over night. Next evening roast the meat 15 minutes per pound in a preheated oven at 350 degrees. Baste occasionally with the juice, and rub the butter on when halfway finished. This will serve 12 and is delicious with wild rice, buttered new potatoes in their jackets, Brussels sprouts, or buttered carrots, a tossed salad and hot rolls.

Here, again, a bottle of Merlot or a decent jug of burgundy would go very well.

VENISON STROGANOFF

My sister-in-law, Jan Hayes, sent me this recipe from the Texas Department of Agriculture. I've tried it and liked it.

2 lb. venison steak (ham steaks, cut from the center of a rear haunch will do just fine)
¾ cup all-purpose flour
½ tsp. salt
½ tsp. black pepper
2 medium onions, sliced and separated into rings
2 cups sliced fresh mushrooms
1 cup boiling water
½ tsp. dry mustard
½ cup sour cream
1 lb. egg noodles
salt and pepper to taste

Slice the venison across the grain into thin strips. Mix flour, salt and pepper in a bag, add venison strips and shake until coated. Melt butter in a large skillet. Brown meat lightly in butter. Add onion rings, mushrooms, water and dry mustard. Cover and cook slowly 1½ to 2 hours or until tender. Stir in sour cream, add salt and pepper to taste. DO NOT boil after sour cream has been added. Serve over cooked noodles.

This doesn't need much else. Maybe a crisp green salad, hot rolls or French bread, and a couple of bottles of ice-cold beer.

GRIZZLY CREEK ELK STEAK

A couple of years ago I was looking for a campsight to use later in the season. I drove into the Grizzly Creek campground high on the Great Divide near the Colorado-Wyoming line. An old gentleman was patiently butchering a fine elk he had taken within 50 yards of the camp. Something that smelled marvelous was bubbling and sputtering in a huge, covered frying pan, set on a grill over the campfire. Here's what it was.

2 or 3 elk steaks or chops (about 2 lbs.)
½ cup red wine
1 small can button mushrooms, sliced
1 can beef broth
1 tbsp. brown sugar
1 garlic clove, minced
2 or 3 whole cloves
1 bay leaf
2 or 3 dashes Worcestershire sauce
1 pinch black pepper
1/8 lb. butter

Melt butter in frying pan, add meat and brown well on both sides. Add all the rest of the ingredients, cover, reduce heat and cook slowly for 2 hours. Remove meat to hot serving platter. Measure the remaining juices and mushrooms, adding water if necessary to make ¾ cup to 1 cup. Return to pan, thicken with corn starch or flour. When bubbling, pour over meat and serve.

In another pot the old man was boiling potatoes. He said when his grown sons got back in from the hunt they would have a couple of bourbons then sit down to elk steaks, mashed potatoes and gravy. Sounded pretty good to me.

ELK STEAKS IN BEER

A friend here in Evergreen, CO, invited me over for an elk dinner a couple of years ago, and it was a marvelous dinner, indeed. When I asked for the recipe he handed me a xerox of what looked like a type-written page out of a community or garden club cookbook done on loose-leaf pages. He didn't remember where he got it. The recipe was credited to a Barbara Phelps of Boulder. I have been unable to locate Ms. Phelps, but hope she will forgive me for using her recipe. It's too good to pass up.

1 can 7-up
1 lb. elk steak
1 tbsp. butter
1 can beer
½ tsp. basil
½ tsp. garlic salt
1 pinch black pepper
1 pkg. brown gravy or mushroom mix
1 tbsp. Worcestershire sauce

Marinate the elk steak in 7-up over night. Then cut it across the grain in thin strips about 2 in. long. Brown in butter in a heavy skillet. Add beer, basil, garlic salt and pepper. Cover and simmer about 45 minutes. Stir in the gravy mix, add Worcestershire sauce and cook another 5 to 10 minutes. Serve over fluffy rice.

We had it with broad egg noodles, broccoli with melted cheese, a crisp salad, and tall, cold bottles of Killian's Irish Red beer.

Thank you Barbara Phelps, wherever you are!

DUTCH OVEN VENISON

Here's one you can set up before you go out in the morning. Cook it in the oven, on top of the stove, or over a camp-fire all day with low to medium heat. It will be scrumptiously ready for dinner.

1 shoulder of venison
1 can beef broth (or one bouillon cube and 1 cup water)
½ cup red wine
1 stick butter
1 tsp. dry mustard
3 tbsp. brown sugar
1 pinch basil
flour, salt, pepper, and garlic salt to taste

Flour and season the roast with pepper, salt and garlic salt. Brown roast in Dutch oven, using half the butter. When browned on all sides and ends, remove roast. Add the rest of the butter and all other ingredients, stirring 'til the butter melts and the ingredients are mixed. Put the roast back in, cover, lower the heat and go hunting or something. Turn the roast over two or three times during the day.

Serve with boiled, mashed, or baked potatoes, gravy, and green vegetable and plenty of good red wine.

VENISON HASENPFEFFER

Here's another of Charlie Stuart's great recipes.

2 lbs. venison
½ cup red wine
1 medium onion, sliced
2 bay leaves
1 tsp. black pepper
½ cup vinegar
½ cup water
1 cup sour cream
2 tbsp. butter
1 tsp. salt

Soak the meat for two days in a solution of water, vinegar, sliced onions, melted butter, bay leaves, salt and pepper. Next, wipe the meat dry and brown it in a Dutch oven in hot butter. Add about a cup of the soaking solution. Cover and simmer 1 ½ to 2 hours, or until the meat is tender. When almost ready to serve, add ½ cup red wine and 1 cup sour cream. Stir well and turn the meat in it several times.

Egg noodles, potato pancakes and cabbage, red or green, go well with this succulent dish.

Mitt beer, Otto!

VENISON SAUERBRATEN

Variations of this recipe can be found in most game cookbooks, which means only that it's a good recipe, and that many people have tried it and liked it. Like any other pot roast, it's a good one for use in a hunting camp; you can set it up during the noon break, put it on the stove, and know you'll have a super dinner ready when you get back in. It works equally well with deer, elk or moose.

3 - 4 lb. shoulder roast
4 - 5 medium onions, quartered
4 - 5 potatoes
1 yellow turnip
4 - 5 carrots
4 stalks celery
1 lb. fresh mushrooms, sliced
2 cups red wine
1 cup beef broth or bouillon
1 cup cider vinegar
1/3 cup lemon juice
3 - 4 garlic cloves
12 juniper berries, crushed
12 pepper corns, green or black
1 bay leaf
3 - 4 whole cloves
1 pinch basil
1 pinch powdered ginger, or 1 in. piece whole ginger
1 tsp. salt
12 - 15 ginger snaps
flour, vegetable oil

Flour the meat and brown it in the vegetable oil in a cast iron Dutch oven. When well browned on all sides and ends, add everything but the mushrooms and ginger snaps. The vegetables should be washed, peeled and cut in fork-sized pieces. Add a couple of dashes of Worcestershire sauce, if you like. Bring the pot to a boil, reduce heat, cover, and simmer for 3 hours, stirring occasionally. At the end of two hours, smell and taste. It should be pungent, and make your mouth pucker a little. Add mushrooms, and the wine, vinegar, lemon juice or water as necessary. Cook one more hour to allow the flavors to blend and to eliminate the raw taste of the added wine.

Crush and roll out the ginger snaps as fine as possible. When the roast is done, remove the meat and vegetables and place them in heated serving dishes. Strain the gravy and juices to remove pepper corns, garlic, juniper berries, etc. Reheat the gravy, adding the crushed ginger snaps, stirring until thickened.

Serve with egg noodles, green or red cabbage, garlic bread, and either dark beer or red wine.

VENISON STEAK AU POIVRE

When I was a youngster, I read someplace that when President Roosevelt's doctors and wife weren't looking, he got the White House Chef to cut him a thick Porterhouse steak, cut some pockets in it, stuff them with black pepper and other spices, soak it in bourbon, and flame broil it—rare and juicy. I've done it that way many times, and love it. Here's a variation for deer, elk or moose steak.

> venison steak (loin, backstrap, or ham) 1 to 1½ in. thick
> fresh, coarse-cracked black pepper
> minced garlic cloves
> dried basil or oregano
> bourbon

Rub both sides of steaks with a split garlic clove. Cut three or four pockets about an inch long and half-inch deep on both sides. Stuff the pockets with freshly cracked pepper, minced garlic and basil or oregano. Soak the steaks in bourbon for 45 minutes. Broil over a charcoal fire (or pan broil in a dry cast iron skillet that's blazing hot) about 3½ to 4 minutes a side for rare meat. When steaks are just about ready, pour more bourbon over them and flame. Serve while they're still sizzling.

A Caesar salad, hot, buttery baked potatoes, and a bottle of red wine top the meal off superbly.

If you don't like the taste of bourbon—rum, Cognac or Irish whiskey work just as well.

CHICKEN FRIED DEER MEAT

There are probably as many recipes for chicken fried steak as there are people who love this southern favorite...which must be in the millions. Served with greens (collard, mustard, turnip, or kale), black-eyed peas, homemade biscuits and currant jelly, or your personal favorites, this traditional recipe is sure to please.

1½ - 2 lbs. round or ham steaks, not more than ½ in. thick
1 egg, beaten
½ cup milk or buttermilk
½ cup flour
3 tbsp. butter
pepper, salt to taste, vegetable oil

Cream Gravy

1½ cups milk, buttermilk, or condensed milk
2 tbsp. butter
2 - 3 tbsp. flour
1 pinch each, pepper, salt, paprika

Cut the meat into pan-sized pieces, removing any bones, fat, or membrane. Pound the hell out of it on a cutting board with one of those meat-tenderizing mallets that looks like an Iron Maiden. If you don't have one, a wooden mallet from your tool box, a piece of broom handle, or the end of a full can of beer will do. (Just don't open it for a while!)

Set up two bowls and a plate, side by side. Mix the milk and egg in the first bowl, and the flour, salt, pepper, and paprika in the second.

Dip the meat in the milk, then in the flour, coating both sides, and set on the plate. Melt the butter and oil in a big skillet and brown the meat on both sides. If you've pounded it thin enough, browning on both sides will cook the meat enough. Set aside. Add the cream gravy ingredients to the pan, stirring all the while, and cook until its thickened. Pour over the meat and serve.

Sometime in the late '60s, after I had moved to Virginia, I rented one of those self-contained camping units to hunt from. It wasn't square, like a Winnebago, but had a Ford or Chevy truck-snoot sticking out in the front, with part of the living quarters over the top of the cab. It had a refrigerator, stove, oven, toilet, and sleeping room for six, if they were all married or at least very good friends.

Anyway, I rented this monster in Fairfax, VA, and headed for New York. I picked up Jim Brown in Jackson Heights, and my wife's cousin, Jimmy Piccione in north Jersey, and headed up Route 17 for Roscoe. My son, J.T., was in college, and was driving down from Lake Geneva to meet us at the campsite.

Things started going wrong the minute we got there. It was bitter cold—around zero—that night. It never got above 12 degrees all week, and it was snowing like hell with maybe a foot and a half of snow already on the ground. We had parked in a clearing on the edge of some great public hunting land, and were unpacking our gear and all the groceries and stuff. I had a half-gallon jug of wine in each hand and was going to put them out in the snow to chill. I slipped on the collapsible step and my feet went out from under me. I didn't dare put my hands down to break the fall for fear of smashing the wine jugs. The base of my spine hit the deck about the same time the back of my skull hit the door jam and I went down for the count. Next thing I knew J.T. was rubbing snow in my face to bring me around, and Jim and Jimmy were helping me up...with a full jug of wine in each hand.

The headache I had was only the first of many that week. The water pipes froze up immediately, the batteries went dead and we had no generator, and it got so cold that the propane thickened up and wouldn't flow to the stoves, so we had no heat. But all that, and more, came later.

That night we had a bunch of Scotch whiskey and beer and wine and such, and I heated up a huge pot of chili I had made at home. It was loaded with jalapeño peppers. I mean, loaded. I had developed quite a tolerance for those little green puppies, but this time I had really outdone myself. Jim Brown quit after two mouthfuls, claiming ulcers, and ate a bottle of Ballantine's for dinner. J.T. followed soon after, gasping for air, and trying to put out the fire with three quick cans of Pepsi.

Cousin Jimmy was game to the end, however, and even had

seconds with me. Man, that chili was hot! We sat there and ate two bowls of it, sweating like crazy, tears running from our eyes, and our sinuses cleared for a month. We washed it down with a lot of everything drinkable.

Next morning, five below zero, light snow falling, and a two-foot blanket of it covering everything. It hardly gets more beautiful than that. We were all dressed for that kind of weather, including Jimmy, who had on a one-piece, blaze-orange snow mobile suit that zipped up from inside the left ankle, clear to the right side of his neck.

Jim was going to still-hunt along the bottom by the creek. J.T., who was still young and had ants in his pants, was going to hunt along the top ridges. I dropped Jimmy off in a likely place about half way up the hill and said I would take a stand further up, and would work my way back down to him about 11 o'clock, it now being about 6:30.

The deer, being smarter than we, were hunkered down someplace, wisely waiting for the storm to blow over.

I didn't see anything all morning but a couple of does, and began to head back down about 10:30. When I got to Jimmy, he was pale, trembling, and cursing loudly and with great vehemence.

"You bastard," he said.

"What did I do. What are you talking about?"

"You and your damned chili," he yelled in my face, shaking his gun at me. "I've had the runs since 8 o'clock. Maybe 20 times I've had to get out of this monkey suit, and every time blue flame shot out of my rear end, and I've defoliated this whole damn mountain, and I'm so burnt I've been using snow on myself to cool it off, and I'm never going to eat your goddamn chili again."

"You think 11 o'clock is too early to have a drink?"

"Hell, no! Let's get out of here. Oh, God! I have to go again."

So don't make your chili too hot. Here's a recipe that should warm you without doing any serious damage to your digestive tract.

VENISON CHILI

Chili is a favorite in most deer camps. Hot, savory and satisfying, it can be kept on the back burner or edge of the campfire, getting better all the time, ready for anyone who wants to ladle out a cup. To be perfectly honest, I cheat...starting out with Wick Fowler's 2-Alarm Chili Mix. It's the best prepared mix of spices I've found, and its available at most supermarkets. They put too much salt in it for my taste, though, and I use only half of what's provided in the little packet. To these ingredients I add:

  2 medium onions, cut up
  2 green peppers, diced
  2 garlic cloves, minced
  6 jalapeño or chili peppers, cut small
  1½ lb. deer, elk or moose meat, cubed, not ground
  ¾ lb. lean pork, cubed
  ½ cup red wine
  1 can chili beans, drained

Follow the directions on the package, adding the additional ingredients, and thickening at the end with maza flour provided in the package. Some folks add beer, brown sugar or molasses, more chili powder or cumin; some leave out the beans. It's your call. The recipe, as is, provides a hearty chili that will warm your insides at a deer camp, or beside the TV on a chilly football Sunday.

VENISON MEATBALLS AND SAUSAGE ITALIAN STYLE

In the section *On Being Camp Cook,* the menu calls for an Italian spaghetti and meatball dinner. Here's the recipe for the meatballs, sausages, and what *real* Italians call gravy! Ground venison, elk, moose, or antelope can be used, as well as ground round or chuck of beef. If you use ground chuck, remember that it's fattier than round. Be sure to drain off all the fat as you brown them.

2 lbs. ground venison
1 lb. sweet Italian sausage without the casings
1 lb. hot Italian sausage links
1 tbsp. fresh, or dried parsley
2 garlic cloves, minced
1 pinch each thyme, oregano, basil, red pepper
1 egg, beaten
¼ cup seasoned bread crumbs
2 tbsp. grated Parmesan or Romano cheese
pepper and salt to taste

Combine all ingredients except the hot sausage links in a bowl and mix thoroughly, using your fingers. The mixture should be wet enough so the meatballs stick together. If it feels too moist, add some more bread crumbs. Put a bowl or pot of hot water convenient to where you're working, and dip your hands in it frequently as you roll out the meatballs about golf-ball size. For some reason (you'll have to ask my mother-in-law), the hot water makes the meatballs more tender, so help me.

Brown the meatballs gently in a little olive oil in a large skillet. Drain on paper towels and set aside. Cut the hot sausage links in pieces about 1½ inches long, and brown them in the skillet. Drain and set aside with the meatballs.

THE GRAVY

2 large cans peeled plum tomatoes
1 small can tomato paste
1 cup red wine
4 tbsp. olive oil
2 garlic cloves, minced
1 generous pinch each of thyme, basil, oregano, and cracked, hot red pepper
2 medium onions, chopped
pepper and salt to taste
one tomato can of water

Combine all ingredients in a large pot and stir thoroughly. Break up the tomatoes with a potato masher. Add meatballs and sausages. Bring to a boil, reduce heat, cover, and simmer for at least two hours. Then, if it's too thin, add another can of tomato paste; if too thick, add water. It should be reasonably thick, and kind of lumpy. Adjust spices as necessary. If you add anything, let it simmer a little longer.

Boil a pound of thin spaghetti, vermicelli, or linguini according to the package directions. Drain and put in a large bowl, add a ladle full of gravy and toss to prevent the pasta from sticking together. Remove the meatballs and sausages, putting them in heated serving dishes or bowls. Skim fat off gravy. Pour some gravy on top of spaghetti, put the rest in a pre-heated gravy boat or serving bowl. Serve everything piping hot, with small dishes of grated Parmesan cheese and cracked red pepper on the side. A crisp green or Caesar salad, hot garlic bread, and a large bottle of Chianti will make this a meal to remember.

*If time, so fleeting, must like humans die,
let it be filled with good food and good talk,
and then embalmed in the perfumes of conviviality.*

M.F.K. Fisher
The Art of Eating

ROAST LEG OF BIG HORN SHEEP

This magnificent critter is perhaps the toughest to bring home of any animal on the North American continent. When cooked he will be to domestic lamb or mutton as elk or deer is to beef...leaner, more muscular, and tasting more like lamb than lamb does.

1 haunch of sheep
5 garlic cloves, peeled but whole
½ stick of butter
1 stick Chef's butter (see p. 36)
pepper, salt, dried rosemary

Wash meat and pat dry with paper towels. Using a Phillips head screwdriver or the pointed end of your sharpening steel, pierce the meat an inch deep in five different places. Stuff these holes with butter, a clove of garlic, and pinch of crushed, dried rosemary. Pepper and salt the outside.

Place on a grill over a hot fire and cook for about two hours, turning every half hour, and rubbing some of the Chef's butter into the surface each time you turn it. Check for "doneness" by taking a slice through the thick part. It may need another half hour or so, but should be medium rare and juicy.

Remove to a hot platter, carve off 5 or 6 slices, arrange on the platter and dot the whole thing with the remaining Chef's butter. Serve with quartered roasted potatoes, buttered Brussels sprouts, mint-apple jelly, and a hearty burgundy.

CURRY OF BIGHORN SHEEP

2 - 3 lb. sheep meat, cut in cubes
2 onions, sliced thin
1 garlic clove, minced
2 ½ cups meat stock, beef broth, or bouillon
2 tbs. curry powder, preferably hot
2 tbs. vinegar
1 bay leaf
1 tbs. allspice
pepper, salt, cayenne pepper, Tabasco sauce, cooking oil

Brown the meat in hot oil in a Dutch oven. Remove and set aside. Cook onion and garlic in the oil over low heat until soft but not brown. Stir in the spices, then the broth and vinegar. Put the meat back in, add the bay leaf and a couple of healthy dashes of Tabasco. Cover and simmer for about two hours, stirring occasionally, until meat is tender. Add more Tabasco, if you like, just before serving. Serve with buttered egg noodles or rice, and plenty of cold beer.

BAKED BEAR CHOPS WITH SAUERKRAUT

Bear meat, like pork, should be thoroughly cooked. And like pork, it has a wonderful flavor and texture, making it well worth the effort. You can substitute loin pork chops for the bear chops in this recipe, just trim off most of the fat.

6 bear chops, or pork loin
4 medium potatoes, sliced thin
2 large onions, sliced thin
2 tart, green apples, cored, peeled and sliced
1 large can sauerkraut, drained
1 cup dry white wine or a can of beer
pepper, salt, caraway seed, flour, vegetable oil

Flour, pepper and salt the chops (shaking them in a paper or plastic bag with 1/3 cup of flour is the best way) and brown them in a large skillet with a little vegetable oil. Drain and place in the bottom of a Dutch oven or large oven-roasting pan. Cover with potatoes, onions, apples and sauerkraut. Add white wine or beer and season with pepper, salt, and a few pinches of caraway seed. Cover and bake in a 350 degree oven for 2 to 2½ hours, until chops are tender. If you don't have a cover for the roasting pan, seal tightly with aluminum foil.

Serve with hot mustard, crunchy dill pickles, sour rye bread, and lots of beer.

ANTELOPE PAPRIGASH

The fleet-footed pronghorn is as much fun to watch as he is hard to hunt and good to eat. In the off season they will frequently allow you to get pretty close to them. On the way back from a fishing trip to Yellowstone a few years ago, I made a pit stop at a rest area outside of Lander, WY. When I came out of the building there were two of them standing there looking at me, not 10 feet away, grazing on the manicured grass. I talked to them softly for a few minutes, and when I walked slowly past them to get to my car, they seemed totally unconcerned. This was before the season opened, of course. Ah, well!

2 lbs. antelope steak or boneless roast
½ cup sherry or red wine
1 cup beef broth or bouillon
1 tbsp. cider vinegar
½ pint sour cream
1 tbsp. Worcestershire sauce
½ tsp. dry mustard
½ lb. fresh mushrooms, sliced
2 shallots or one medium onion, sliced thin
flour, butter, cooking oil, pepper, salt, paprika, Tabasco sauce

Slice the meat into pan-sized pieces. Put about 1/3 cup of flour, a teaspoon each of pepper, salt and paprika in a paper or plastic bag. Shake to mix. Add meat and shake to coat. Melt a little butter and cooking oil in a skillet and brown the meat on both sides, shaking on a little more paprika.

Place browned meat in an oven roasting pan or pyrex lasagna dish with cover. Cover with mushrooms and shallots. Mix sherry, beef broth, vinegar, dry mustard and Worcestershire sauce in a bowl, adding a couple of dashes of Tabasco. Pour over meat, cover or seal with foil, and bake in a 350 degree oven for 2 hours. Remove meat and mushrooms from pan with slotted spoon and put in a pre-heated serving bowl or deep dish. Put roasting pan on the stove over a medium low heat. Stir sour cream into liquid, mixing thoroughly until heated through. Don't let it boil, as the sour cream will begin to separate and look terrible. Pour gravy over meat and serve with rice or egg noodles.

This recipe works well with rabbit, squirrel, or game birds, substituting chicken broth for the beef, and dry white wine for the sherry.

SAGE SAUSAGE

2 lbs. ground deer, elk or moose meat
¾ lb. chopped raw bacon or prepared pork sausage
2 tsp. dried sage, finely crushed
1 tsp. black pepper
1 tsp. Worcestershire sauce

Place all ingredients in a bowl and mix thoroughly. Use your hands; get down and dirty and really smush it up well. Shape into patties and fry until browned on both sides and well done.

Serve with screwdrivers or Bloody Marys, scrambled eggs, toast, coffee, and the Sunday paper.

Stack leftover (uncooked) patties about 6 deep, separating them with pieces of waxed paper. Put the stack in a zip-lock bag, squeezing the air out of it as you close it, and freeze for another day. Cooked leftovers can be reheated as sausage sandwiches for lunch.

BUTTERMILK ROAST ELK

A rich gravy, thickened with buttermilk or sour cream adds an elegant touch to any wild roast, from deer and elk to pheasant and duck. Try this one with a hunk of that walking hat-rack you finally bagged.

1 4-5 lb. shoulder roast of elk, moose or deer
2 medium onions, sliced
2 garlic cloves, minced
10 juniper berries, crushed
1 pkg. onion soup mix
1 qt. buttermilk
flour, pepper, salt, cooking oil

Flour the roast and sprinkle it with pepper and salt. Brown in cooking oil and put in an oven-roasting pan or Dutch oven. Cover with onions. Mix garlic, juniper berries, onion soup mix and buttermilk, and pour over roast. Cover and cook in 350 degree oven 2½ to 3 hours. When done, remove roast to hot platter, stir pan juices and gravy, thickening if necessary with a little corn starch and water. Strain, pour over sliced meat and serve.

For a variation, omit juniper berries, and add 2 tbsp. currant jelly when stirring gravy.

GAME STEAKS ITALIANO

Here's an easy way to cook a couple of "ham" steaks cut off a haunch of elk or moose. Do it on top of the stove in a big skillet, and have a couple of drinks. There's hardly any way you can screw it up.

2 inch-thick ham steaks of elk or moose
2 garlic cloves, minced
2 onions, sliced
1 pinch each, thyme, basil, oregano
1 jar spaghetti sauce
pepper, salt, flour, cooking oil

Pound the steaks pretty good with a mallet or some such, then flour, salt and pepper them. Brown in a little hot oil. Drain the excess oil, add the rest of the ingredients, cover and simmer about an hour and a half until the meat is tender.

Serve with a side order of linguini, Parmesan cheese, and a bottle of Chianti. Salud!

One year Jim Brown and I arranged our schedules so we could hunt opening day—the first in some years—and even took a Friday afternoon off so we could get up to John Schwanneger's place for dinner and to plan the next day's hunt. It was a lovely drive, and the Catskills were all golden and flame as the hardwoods turned color, and we were warmed with Scotch whiskey and good feeling.

There were to be 13 of us in all, and as we sat down to a table laden with heaping platters of fresh venison chops, saddle, a roast haunch, mashed potatoes, gravy, and turnip greens, our host said,

"Perhaps you shentlemen iss vonderink how come ve got all ziss frresh deer meat to eat tonight, und zer season doesn't open 'til tommorrrow. Vell, you see, zer deers like to come down at night from zer mountain und feed on zer apples in mine orchard. Und last night, vun of zem falls out from an apple trrree und brrreaks hiss leg, und I haff to shoot him to put him out uff hiss misery. It vass an act uff pure mercy on my part. So enshoy it. Prosit!"

Whether John had gotten a little "camp meat" prematurely, or had taken the deer during the earlier archery season I had not the temerity to ask, but I will never forget that marvelous dinner.

Afterwards, after second helpings of everything, including hot apple pie with ice cream, and lots of fresh coffee, we were directed by our host ..."to zer librrrarrry for brrandy und cigars und a dizcussion frrom tomorrrrows hunt." The air was soon blue with cigar smoke and heavy with the smell of Cognac and Grand Marnier on our collective breaths. Two topo maps, cut and pasted together were spread out on a big table, and marked with 13 Xs.

"Shentlemen," says himself, "If you vill gazzer arrround zer table, I haff developed a plan. If zer Fuhrer had seen ziss plan, he vould haff made me a Field Marshall. (John and his family left Germany in 1929, so his knowledge of the Fuhrer was a little slim.)

"Ziss iss my mountain, und I know it more better zan zer back uff my foot. Ve gonna each take a shpot by an X in zer dark shtill, und ve gonna vait...mitt patience. Und prrrety soon all zem Sears und Rrrroebuck hunters from ze Antrim Lotch gonna come banging und crrrashing through zer voods, und falling down, und makin 'sound shots', und blowing vistles, und zey gonna drrrive zem deers rrrrright into out leps. You betcha!"

We were all—dutifully—on our appointed stands before dawn, and sure enough, soon after first light we heard them. From the Antrim Lodge, from every motel in Roscoe, and from trailer parks and campsites in between, they did, indeed, come crashing through the woods. It was about 6:40. By 9 o'clock, nine of us had our bucks, four spikes, three 4-pointers, one 3 by 4, and one 8-pointer...all on the spots that John had marked. The other four got theirs bucks within two days. What a hunt!

DEER ROAST WITH ROCKY MOUNTAIN KOOL-AID

Beer can make an old pot roast taste pretty special. Here's a favorite deer camp recipe.

1 4-5 lb. shoulder or rump roast
2 cans Coors (or Bud, or Old Frothingslosh)
1 can beef broth (or bouillon and water)
2 medium onions, chopped fine
3 garlic cloves, minced
1 good pinch each, parsley, thyme, basil
½ lb. fresh mushrooms, sliced
10 juniper berries, crushed
1 bay leaf
flour, cooking oil, salt, pepper

Flour and season the roast with salt and pepper. Brown thoroughly with a little cooking oil in a Dutch oven. Mix the rest of the ingredients in a bowl, and pour over the meat. Bring to a boil. Reduce heat, cover and simmer 2 to 2½ hours or until meat is tender. Remove meat to hot platter. Strain gravy and return to pot. Thicken with a little flour or cornstarch in water. Pour over sliced meat, and serve with boiled potatoes or egg noodles, a vegetable of choice and a lot more beer.

VENISON MEAT LOAF WITH MUSHROOMS AND WINE

A tasty meat loaf with plenty of gravy and mashed potatoes is a hearty meal for home or camp. In the unlikely event that there is any left over, a cold meat loaf sandwich on fresh white bread with lots of catsup is to die for.

3 lbs. ground venison
1 lb. ground pork sausage
1 can cream of mushroom soup, undiluted
1 can button mushrooms, sliced
1 onion, chopped fine
1 pinch each, parsley, thyme, basil
2 cups seasoned bread crumbs
1 egg, beaten
1 can beef broth or bouillon
1 pkg. mushroom gravy mix
pepper and salt to taste

Mix the packaged gravy mix and the beef broth in a bowl and set aside. Combine all other ingredients, mix thoroughly by hand, and shape into a loaf. Put in a roasting pan or Dutch oven. Pour the gravy mix and broth over the top. Cover and cook 45 minutes in a 325 degree oven. Uncover and cook another 30 minutes.

Slice loaf and arrange on hot serving platter, pour gravy over it and serve with hot buttered mashed potatoes, fresh string beans and a bottle of red wine.

VENISON PICCATA

5 lb. thin sliced venison, elk, or moose
1 cup lemon juice
1 whole lemon
1 stick butter
¼ cup Marsala, or white wine
flour, pepper and salt to taste, fresh parsley

Soak the sliced meat overnight in a solution of 1/3 each water, white wine, and vinegar. Pour off the liquid and dry the meat with paper towels. Then soak the meat in 1 cup of lemon juice for about an hour. Remove and flour the meat, seasoning it lightly with pepper and salt. Sauté in butter until brown. Sprinkle with fresh, chopped parsley while cooking. Arrange on a hot platter with thin slices of fresh lemon. Pour the Marsala and a squeeze of lemon into the hot pan drippings. Add more butter if necessary. Stir and heat till bubbling. Pour over the meat and serve with sliced buttered zucchini, a salad, and chilled white wine.

(The following recipe is reprinted in it's entirety - including the introduction - from Charlie Stuart's fine cookbook that Country Publishers issued a few years ago. Mr. Stuart is obviously my kind of man. JJH)

VENISON COURVOISIER

"Several years ago I was getting ready to cook some venison round. I had cut about 4 pounds of meat into bite-sized chunks. I melted a tablespoon of butter in a red hot skillet and added the meat. While doing this I had been drinking a bit of Cognac to warm the system. Why not a little brandy for the meat? I put in a jigger (1½ ounces), stirred it, and tasted the result. Delicious—it made the meat very succulent. I added two more ounces, had a couple myself, and finished cooking the meat. Wild rice and salad completed the meal. The same procedure can be followed for elk, moose, caribou, or big horn sheep." I bet!

4 lbs. venison round
3 oz. Cognac or brandy
½ tbsp. cracked pepper
1 tbsp. butter
1 tsp. salt

If you know the venison is tough, sprinkle meat tenderizer over it an hour before cooking. Cut meat into bite-sized chunks. Get skillet very hot. Add butter, then the meat, Cognac, salt and pepper to taste. Cook quickly and stir constantly.

And have a couple of snorts for Charlie.

For venison and other big game stew recipes, see the *Stews and Soups* section beginning on p. 126.

*Sharing food with another human being
is an intimate act
that should not be indulged in lightly.*

M.F.K. Fisher
The Art of Eating

My son, J.T., was about 13 when I took him deer hunting for the first time. Jim Brown was with us, and we were hunting out of my mother's old farm house near South Royalton, VT. It was all rolling hills, dairy farm country, and the corn-fed deer were fat and plentiful. It was cold, and the woods were wet with sleet and freezing rain.

I put the youngster on a stand at the edge of some hardwoods where there was a good view back down the mountain toward the thick hemlocks and alders along the banks of the brook. I told him to stay put and keep his eyes open; that I would circle way around, and drive through the creek-bottom. In that weather there was a good chance that a deer was hunkered down under a hemlock along the brook, and maybe I could kick him up toward the stand.

It was still half-dark as I walked back out of the woods along an old logging road, and I spotted Jim Brown working his way up the ridge to a favorite stand. I had a smoke and waited for full daylight. I heard a buck snort somewhere in there, and the woods were beautiful, even in the freezing rain.

It was tough, wet going, slogging through the thick cover of the creek bottom, and in spite of my rain gear, I was soon soaked through to the skin. But sure enough, as I approached a spot below where I had left J.T., a nice spikehorn exploded out from under a big hemlock and bolted up the hill toward the stand. I expected to hear a shot any minute, and was excited at the prospect of the boy getting a nice buck on his first time out. I heard only the wet silence of the woods, and my own heart pounding from exertion.

Following the deer's tracks through the wet leaves, I saw that he passed within 30 yards of where I had left my son, who was now nowhere in sight. I was furious. I caught up with him a half-hour later and asked him where he was when the buck ran by. He said he got "bored" sitting there and decided to wander up to the top of the mountain. I dressed him out pretty severely about his responsibility to other hunters, about being where he was supposed to be, and about not leaving his stand until the drive was over.

"You're grounded for the rest of the day," I finished. "Unload your rifle and go back to the house." A little harsh, I knew, but he'd never learn any quicker.

That's not quite the end of the story, though. The following year the three of us returned to Vermont for the last week of the season, right after Thanksgiving. It was bitter cold, snowy, and windy, and it didn't lend itself to any long-term stand sitting, so I didn't plan a drive. Jim was going to still-hunt up along the ridge, and I suggested to J.T. that he try that old stand for a while, and that I'd catch up to him later. It was about 6:30 and so cold that the moisture froze in your nose. I didn't see anybody for several hours.

About 11:30 I built a fire in a clear spot in the logging road, and was warming myself beside it with a thermos of hot coffee, when Jim showed up.

"You better get J.T.," he said. "I just passed him on that old stand of yours. He's blue with the cold, his teeth are chattering so hard he can hardly talk, and he's shaking all over. I tried to talk him into coming with me, but he said he couldn't leave the stand until you told him to."

God, kids can sure make you feel guilty sometimes.

UPLAND GAME—BUNNIES AND BIRDS

As popular as deer hunting is in America, there are many more folks by far, who enjoy going into the field in the early fall in search of rabbits, squirrels, and the numerous varieties of game birds that seem to thrive over much of the land. The sight of a kid with a .22 or single-shot 20 gauge over his shoulder and a couple of cottontails hanging from his belt was a pretty common occurrence when I was growing up. (I wonder what ever happened to "the sweet 16?") It still is in much of the country.

Though the urbanization of America has reduced both the habitat these creatures need and the human population living in "the country," the animals and the desire to hunt them seem to have survived admirably, even near big cities. Over the years I have successfully hunted rabbits, squirrels and pheasants within sight of Manhattan skyscrapers.

In spite of our best efforts to screw them up, wetlands and flyways still provide us access to ducks, geese and other water fowl. It's not as good as in the old days, of course...but then, nothing is, including you or me.

Herewith, then, recipes for our smaller furred and feathered friends. A lot of game cookbooks call for cooking small game in pressure cookers (they make tender squirrels and rabbits) or crock pots. I've had a couple of pressure cookers blow up on me, through my own or someone else's carelessness, and avoid them like the plague. I prefer a Dutch oven to a crock pot, so there you are.

Many recipes for rabbit are interchangeable with squirrel as well as many game birds. Don't be afraid to experiment, remembering only that squirrel tends to be a little tougher, and may require longer cooking.

As with the section on big game, I've omitted stews and soups here, and have included them in their own section.

BAKED RABBIT PAPRIKA

This is my all-time favorite. If you don't care for the flavor of paprika, leave it out and not great harm is done. The rabbit will still be tender and delicious, though it will obviously lose that distinctive Hungarian flavor.

2 rabbits, washed and cut up
½ cup dry white wine
1 cup chicken broth or bouillon
1 tbsp. vinegar
½ pint sour cream
1 tbsp. Worcestershire sauce
½ tsp. dry mustard
½ lb. fresh mushrooms, sliced
2 shallots or one medium onion, sliced thin
flour, butter, cooking oil, pepper, salt, paprika, Tabasco sauce

Put rabbit pieces, flour, pepper, salt, and a generous amount of paprika in a paper or plastic bag. Shake to mix and coat. Put some butter and/or cooking oil in a skillet, and brown the rabbit pieces on both sides over medium heat, shaking on a little more paprika.

Place browned rabbit in an oven-roasting pan or pyrex lasagna dish with cover. Cover with sliced mushrooms and shallots. Mix white wine, chicken broth, vinegar, dry mustard and Worcestershire sauce in a bowl, adding a couple of dashes of Tabasco sauce. Pour over meat, cover or seal with foil, and bake in a 350 degree oven for 2 hours.

Remove meat and mushrooms from pan with a slotted spoon and put in a pre-heated serving bowl or deep dish. Put roasting pan on the stove over medium low heat. When the liquid starts to bubble, stir in sour cream, mixing thoroughly until heated through. Try not to let it boil, as the sour cream will begin to separate and look terrible. Pour gravy over meat and serve with buttered egg noodles.

If you like this one, try it with cut up frying chicken, grouse, quail, or partridge. A chilled Chardonnay goes down well with it.

BUNNY BARBECUE

Rabbit lends itself to oven barbecueing. It moistens and tenderizes while adding the zest of a good barbecue sauce. Your favorite store-bought sauce will do fine, or you can concoct your own. Here's one that works well.

1 cup catsup
1 can tomato paste
½ cup red wine
2 tbsp. prepared hot mustard
¼ cup Worcestershire sauce
¼ cup honey
salt, pepper, garlic salt, and Tabasco sauce to taste

Stir well and cook for 10 or 15 minutes.

Cut up two rabbits or four squirrels and put in a roasting pan. Pour plenty of the barbecue sauce over the top, and bake in a 325 - 350 degree oven for two hours, turning the pieces occasionally. You can achieve much the same result with a big skillet on the grill over a charcoal fire.

A crisp salad with blue cheese dressing, corn on the cob, and cold beer finish if off. Since there's a natural desire to eat the rabbit meat with your fingers, plenty of napkins are in order.

For a variation, omit the honey and garlic salt, add 2 cloves of minced garlic, a chopped onion, a chopped green pepper, and ¼ cup brown sugar.

RABBIT CORDON BLEU (Sort of)

Chicken breasts Cordon Bleu has always been one of my favorite dishes, particularly when it can be ordered in a good restaurant. Here's a variation for rabbit, squirrel or game birds that can be done easily in camp or at home.

2 rabbits, washed and cut up
½ lb. sliced cheddar or Monterey Jack
½ lb. sliced baked or boiled ham
1 stick butter
pepper, salt, flour to coat

Mix flour, pepper and salt in a bag. Shake rabbit pieces in the bag to coat. Sauté the floured rabbit in the butter until all the pieces are well browned on all sides, at least 10 minutes on each side. If you have an oven, turn the broiler on. Put the rabbit pieces in a broiler pan, cover each piece with a slice of ham, then put the sliced cheese on top, and broil for 5 minutes, or until the cheese is thoroughly melted. If you are cooking on a campfire or a less sophisticated cook stove, cover the rabbit pieces with the ham and cheese as above, right in the fry pan or Dutch oven, or whatever you used, cover it and simmer until the cheese is melted.

Some home fries, a non-broccoli green veggie, and cold beer go well with this one.

BRAISED RABBIT WITH MUSHROOMS

2 rabbits, cut up
1 can cream of mushroom soup
1 can chicken broth
2 medium onions, sliced thin
½ lb. mushrooms, sliced
1 pinch thyme
flour, salt, generous pepper, butter/oil

Combine flour, salt, plenty of pepper in a bag. Shake to mix. Add rabbit and shake to coat. Melt a glob of butter and a little oil in a skillet and brown the rabbit pieces on both sides. Place in a Dutch oven, and cover with sliced onions and mushrooms. Dilute the mushroom soup with the chicken broth (or milk, if you like), sprinkle with thyme and a little more pepper and salt. Cover and bake in a 350 degree oven for an hour and a half. When the rabbit is done, remove to heated serving dish. Thicken the pot juices with a little flour or corn starch mixed with water. Stir well and pour over rabbit.

Serve with home fries and a green vegetable.

BR'ER RABBIT

When I was a kid, Br'er Rabbit and the other stories of Joel Chandler Harris were very popular, and we always used Br'er Rabbit brand molasses in our house for baked beans and I don't know what all. Anyway, here's a recipe for rabbit in molasses, of whatever brand.

    2 rabbits, cut up and washed
    2 onions, chopped
    2 tsp. pepper
    2 tsp. salt
    1 pinch basil
    1/3 cup molasses
    1 cup water
    ¼ cup vinegar
    1 garlic clove, minced

Season the rabbit pieces with the pepper and salt, rubbing it in and all over the meat. Put the meat in a Dutch oven, add the onion and garlic. Mix the molasses, water and vinegar in a bowl, pour over the meat, cover and simmer for about an hour, basting and turning the pieces frequently, until the rabbit is tender and has picked up the color of the molasses. Serve with buttered rice or egg noodles, and some pickled beets.

RABBIT CACCIATORE

My mother-in-law is one of the great cooks in the western world, and produces a chicken cacciatore (hunter style) that could make a statue break out in a smile. Here's a version of that dish for any small game—furred or feathered.

2 rabbits, cut up
1 stick butter
4 tbsp. olive oil
2 stalks celery, chopped
2 carrots, chopped
2 onions, chopped
1 tsp. parsley flakes
1 pinch each, basil and oregano
1 cup dry red wine
½ cup stock or bouillon
½ can tomato paste
pepper and salt to taste

Soak the rabbit pieces in cold water and a couple of tablespoons of salt for about 4 hours. Pat dry. Melt the butter and olive oil in a Dutch oven over medium heat, brown the rabbit pieces on all sides. Reduce heat, add veggies, season to taste, cover and simmer for 10 - 15 minutes. Mix the tomato paste, wine, and stock and stir it into the pot. Cover and simmer for about an hour, stirring occasionally. Add more stock if it gets too thick.

Serve with a side order of linguini tossed in butter, pepper, salt, and a little Parmesan cheese. Red wine, naturally, complements this meal.

JUGGED HARE EMPRESS

Early in World War II, money and meat were equally scarce. The wartime economy had not yet catapulted us out of the depression and times were a little lean for many. Mrs. M.K.F. Fisher, even then an accomplished cook and author, wrote a charming book entitled *How To Cook A Wolf,* (as in, how to keep the wolf from the door). It was filled with good recipes for cheap eats, tips on such things as how to make your own soap, and all mannner of cheerfully presented good advice for living in hard times.

Among the recipes was this one for jugged hare.

How To Cook A Wolf, along with four other of Mrs. Fisher's earlier works, has been reissued by Vintage Books division of Random House, under the title *The Art of Eating.* It's available in paperback in most good bookstores and is wonderful reading. Mrs. Fisher, now 84, is still writing about food and people and cooking and love, and is, undeniably, America's Empress of the Epicurean. Here then, with her gracious permission, and retitled in her honor, JUGGED HARE EMPRESS.

1 large or two small rabbits
1 cup sour cream
water
vinegar or wine
1 onion, sliced
salt, pepper, cloves, bay leaf
butter
oil

Cut up the rabbit and lay in a crock or jar. Cover with equal parts of water and either vinegar or wine; add the onion and spices. Allow this to soak two days, turning the meat at least once.

Remove the meat and brown thoroughly in a mixture of oil and butter. When it is well browned, cover gradually with the pickling sauce, as much as you want. Let it simmer about a half-hour, or until tender. Before serving, stir the sour cream into it.

Back in the late '50s my brother Mark and I were returning from an unsuccessful day of deer hunting near the old mines outside South Royalton, VT. As we trudged down a logging road, the snow crunching softly beneath our boots, a big snowshoe jack rabbit hopped out of a thicket and sat right in the middle of the trail about 50 yards in front of us. We stopped short and I raised the old bolt-action Enfield 30.06 I was hunting with in those days.

"Even if you hit him—which I doubt—that 30.06 ain't going to leave much, " Mark whispered.

"Bullfeathers, " I replied, or something very much like it, "I'll hit him in the head," which, by the most outrageous good luck, was exactly what happened. (My brother still thinks I'm a good shot.)

When we got to him we found that the 180 grain Core-Lokt had neatly decapitated him. He was huge. For years we referred to him as The Headless Horseman. I gutted him and we trudged on home, visions of succulent, tender rabbit dancing in our heads. Skinned out, that sucker weighed nearly 6 lbs.

You've heard the old saw about cooking a hare for three days, throwing it out and eating the pot? That's about what happened.

We fried, baked, broiled, boiled and stewed that puppy and never did get any edible or even chewable result.

If I'd known anything about jugged hare, fricasseeing, or any of the other slow cooking methods in those days, we might not have wasted that fine old Thumper.

Here are a couple of recipes that will bail you out if you suspect the catch of the day is a little long in the tooth.

FRICASSEE OF VARYING HARE

1 or 2 rabbits, or a hare, cut up
1 stick butter
1 can chicken broth or bouillon
1 stalk celery, chopped
1 medium onion, chopped
1 carrot, cut up
1 generous pinch each, parsley and thyme
1 scant pinch sage
1 pkg. turkey gravy mix
flour, pepper, salt

Put flour, pepper and salt in a plastic bag and shake to mix. Add rabbit and shake to coat. Brown the meat in hot butter and a little oil, either in a deep skillet or Dutch oven. Add remaining ingredients, cover and simmer for about 2 hours or until the rabbit gives up and becomes tender. Remove rabbit and vegetables with slotted spoon and place in a pre-heated serving dish. Add gravy mix to pot liquor, stir and simmer for about 2 minutes. Add more broth if necessary. Pour over meat and serve.

Buttered egg noodles and hot biscuits go well with this. There's a fine recipe for easy drop biscuits on the Bisquick box. Don't forget the chilled white wine.

HASENPFEFFER

4 - 5 lbs. rabbit or hare, cut up
1 cup red wine or vinegar
1 cup water or chicken broth
2 onions, sliced
2 cups sour cream
3 or 4 whole cloves
½ stick of butter
1 tsp. each, pepper and salt
1 bay leaf

Combine all ingredients except the wine and sour cream. Soak the meat in the solution for at least two days, turning it occasionally. Dry the meat and brown it well in hot butter. Add ¾ cup of the solution, cover and simmer for about 2 hours, or until the meat is tender. Add red wine and sour cream, stir and serve.

Young rabbits, or squirrels, can be cooked very much like young chickens; fried, sautéed, grilled, or broiled over an open fire. Unlike their older cousins, they don't need to be jugged, crocked, marinated, stewed, or what have you. For campfire grilling or broiling, spit them on a green stick or long fork, rub them with a little butter and pepper and salt, and broil slowly until tender, whole or cut up. With the stars, a couple of pals, and a little Jim Beam for company, simple fare doesn't get much better.

Here are a couple of easy recipes for pan frying.

FRIED RABBIT I

1 or 2 rabbits, cut up
1 large onion, cut up
1 pinch thyme or basil
1 stick butter
flour, pepper and salt

Mix flour, pepper, salt and thyme in a plastic bag, add rabbit pieces and shake to coat. Brown the rabbit pieces on both sides in melted butter over medium heat. Add onion, reduce heat and continue frying for another 10 minutes or so, until the onions are soft. Stir and turn the pieces frequently, adding a little water, butter, or bouillon as necessary to keep from sticking.

Serve with home-fries, buttered broccoli, and a cold beer.

FRIED RABBIT II

1 or 2 rabbits, cut up
1 stick butter
2 pinches parsley
pepper, salt, lemon juice (fresh or bottled)

Soak the rabbit pieces in a half-cup of lemon juice for a half hour or so, turning frequently. Drain them, sprinkle with pepper, salt and parsley, and fry in butter until golden brown and tender, shpritzing on a little more lemon juice from time to time.

Steamed fresh asparagus, a crisp salad with oil and vinegar, and chilled white wine will go well with this.

BAKED GARLIC WITH 12 PIECES OF RABBIT

My friend Jack Mannion, renaissance man, raconteur, and a chef and a half, gave me a recipe of James Beard's called, *Chicken With 40 Cloves of Garlic*. I thought it was a gag. 40 cloves of garlic? Holy Mother!

But I tried it, and of course it was wonderful; neither Beard nor Mannion being dummies.

I've reworked it a little for rabbit, and believe it would be just as excellent with quail, grouse, or partridge.

    2 or 3 rabbits, cut up
    ½ cup olive oil
    2 or 3 stalks of celery, cut up
    2 medium onions, cut up
    2 tsp. salt
    ½ tsp. pepper
    3 tsp. dried parsley flakes, or 6 sprigs fresh
    1 tsp. tarragon
    ½ cup white wine or decent sherry
    40 cloves whole, unpeeled garlic

Put the rabbit pieces in a bowl, pour in the oil, and make sure each piece gets well coated. In a large casserole, lasagna dish, or Dutch oven, combine celery, onion, parsley and tarragon. Lay the rabbit pieces on top. Add the wine and sprinkle with pepper and salt. Tuck the unpeeled garlic cloves in and around and between the meat. Seal tightly with foil *and* a cover, if there is one, and bake in a 350 degree oven for an hour and a half.

The garlic hulls will harden when cooked. Spread the soft insides on slices of Italian or French bread, sop up the juice and enjoy a rare treat. Eat the rabbit, too.

RABBIT MARENGO

I don't remember if Napoleon visited Marengo on his way to Russia, or on the way back, or if he went there specifically to beat up on the Italians. In any case, he kicked butt and, so the story goes, his chef prepared a victory dinner of chicken cooked with local veggies. The recipe comes down to us as *Chicken Marengo*.

Here it is for rabbit, or any of the white meat game birds.

2 rabbits, cut up
2 medium onions, sliced
2 pinches each, oregano, parsley, and basil
1 lg. can peeled, cooked tomatoes
1 bay leaf
½ lb. mushrooms, sliced
¼ cup red wine
1 garlic clove, minced
olive oil, flour, pepper and salt

Put flour, pepper and salt in a bag. Shake to mix. Add rabbit and shake to coat. Brown the rabbit pieces in a little olive oil in a deep skillet, electric frying pan, or Dutch oven. Drain excess oil, add all other ingredients, stir well and bring to a boil. Reduce heat, cover, and simmer for 1 ½ hours or until meat is tender. Stir occasionally. Remove all ingredients and place in a pre-heated serving dish or bowl.

My wife always served broccoli with this; but then, she served broccoli with everything. A green vegetable of your choice, boiled potatoes, and red wine make it a nice meal.

To be honest, I've never shot, cooked, or eaten possum, woodchuck, or raccoon. From reading practically every other game cookbook ever written, I gather that young ones can be pan fried or broiled like young rabbits or squirrels; older ones crocked, jugged, or wet cooked in casserole dishes or Dutch ovens. If so, the preceding recipes should work well for them. I leave that to your discretion, and pass on to a few special birds and waterfowl that I know something about.

ROAST STUFFED WILD TURKEY - A NARRATIVE RECIPE

Wash the bird thoroughly, inside and out, wrap in a damp towel and put him back in the fridge while you take care of the stuffing and the gravy stock. You'll need the heart, liver, gizzard, and neck, so remove and wash them. Cut the neck in three pieces.

Put the organs and neck pieces in a good-sized sauce pan. Add 4 or 5 cups of water and a half-cup of white wine, two stalks of celery cut up, one large onion, quartered, a bay leaf, pepper, salt, two pinches of thyme, and a scant pinch of sage. Bring to a boil, reduce heat, cover, and simmer for an hour and a half. Have a drink.

When the stock has about a half hour to go, chop up 2 stalks of celery and 2 onions nice and fine, and sauté in a big glob of butter. Add pepper and salt and a half-pound of sliced mushrooms.

Stir and cook over medium heat until the onions appear transparent. Don't let them brown. Put everything in the biggest mixing bowl you can find, or in the big pot you use for boiling spaghetti.

Add a large package of seasoned croutons, or prepared bread stuffing mix. Melt a stick of butter, and make another drink.

Remove the heart, liver and gizzard from the stock, cool them under running water, pat dry and chop up on a cutting board. Add to the stuffing mix, along with the melted butter.

Add pepper, salt, and a good pinch or two of sage, moisten with stock and mix well. You want it moist, not sopping wet.

If you like, omit the organ meats, or save them to chop up for the gravy, or throw them out. You can add cooked venison sausage at this point, or cooked chestnuts, or a quart of oysters in their liquor, or don't add anything. Stuff the bird loosely, sealing the cavity with a metal skewer. You can stuff the neck cavity, too.

Rub Mr. Gobbler all over his body with softened butter and put him on a rack in an oven roasting pan. Put a couple of strips of raw bacon on top. Sprinkle with pepper and salt and a pinch or two of thyme.

Make a tent out of a big sheet of heavy-duty aluminum foil. Cover the bird and seal the foil on the ends of the pan. Seal the sides loosely, or not at all. Put in the oven, pre-heated to 350 degrees and roast about 20 - 25 minutes per pound, stuffed. A 10-12 lb. bird should be cooked in about 3½ - 4 hours. Check by taking a cut where the leg meets the side. It should be juicy, but not bloody, or even pink. Remove the foil for the last hour to let his nibs get brown. Remove from oven when done, and set aside while you prepare the gravy.

Strain the remaining stock. Use about 2 cups, add pan drippings, and a package of French's turkey gravy mix. Thicken with a little corn starch mixed with water, if necessary. Stir and simmer for 3 or 4 minutes till you get the consistency you want. Pour into a pre-heated gravy boat or bowl. Remove stuffing to pre-heated serving dish. Turkey should be ready to carve by now. Serve with mashed potatoes and turnips, a green vegetable, candied yams, and a chilled Chardonnay.

It beats the hell out of store-bought turkey.

Noted outdoor artist and writer Russell Chatham once wrote that all game should be cooked and served blood rare, including ducks. Never at a loss for a strongly-held opinion, Chatham went on to say if you don't *like* it that way, you should stick to corned beef hash! In his wonderfully funny story, *The Great Duck Misunderstanding*, Chatham talks about getting drunk, cooking the ducks (barely), and eating them, the gravy and blood running down his arms to the elbows. Yuucchhk! That's where Chatham and I part company.

Elk, moose, deer, antelope, and anything in the sheep and goat families, I like medium-rare to rare, but I can't get bloody fowl past my eyeballs. The recipes that follow allow you to cook your grouse, pheasant, pats or ducks so they are juicy, but bloodless. Adjust according to your taste.

ROAST GOOSE WITH FRUIT GRAVY

The big honkers are wonderful eating, but they get a hell of a lot of exercise, flying back and forth to Canada all the time, and can be tough and dry. Moist cooking methods work best. You can use the bread stuffing used in the roast turkey recipe above, a corn bread stuffing, or a rice stuffing. Here's a recipe that has worked well for me over the years.

Stuffing
1 medium onion, chopped
2 stalks celery, chopped
½ lb. mushrooms, sliced
½ cup white wine
1 box Uncle Ben's Long Grain and Wild Rice Mix
heart, liver, gizzard, pepper, salt, thyme

Prepare the Uncle Ben's rice mix according to directions, substituting ½ cup white wine for ½ cup of the water called for. Sauté the heart, liver and gizzard in butter and a little white wine for 10 - 15 minutes over medium heat, then add onion, celery and mushrooms. Continue cooking until the onion appears transparent. Season with pepper, salt and a pinch of thyme. When done, allow to cool. Remove heart, liver and gizzard, chop up fine. Now combine all ingredients, mix, and stuff the bird loosely. Rub the goose with softened butter, place on a rack in an oven roasting pan. Sprinkle with pepper, salt and a pinch of thyme.

Pan Gravy
1 cup orange juice
½ jar orange marmalade
1 small can mandarin orange slices
1 tsp. Worcestershire sauce
¼ cup white wine
1 can bing cherries, pitted
4 tbsp. red currant jelly

Combine ingredients, pour over bird and into pan. Cover pan tightly, or seal with an aluminum foil tent. Roast at 350 degrees for 2½-3 hours, depending on the dressed, stuffed weight. To test for "doneness," insert a knife blade into the leg joint. It should not be bloody. Cook uncovered for the last hour to brown the goose. When done, remove from pan and set aside for 10 minutes. Thicken pan juices and fruit with a package of brown gravy mix, adding flour if necessary. Chinese stir-fried vegetables go well with the goose and rice stuffing.

I hear the quiet rustling of reeds on the water and the lapping of water on the decoys set so carefully. I hear the restless silence of the hunters in their blind. Way off in the distance I hear the quacking of ducks. As it grows nearer I hear the hunters ready their shotguns. Joined in with the quacking now, is the faint fluttering of wings. Then comes the shotgun blasts, shattering the world all around. I hear the splash of the dog, swimming eagerly to retrieve a bird. I hear the quiet rustling of reeds on the water.

Chris Lamson, Age 13
November, 1983

For nearly 30 years, Wally Bennett was White House photographer for Time magazine, covering the White House and its occupants' doings from Eisenhower on down. (Some say he started with Lincoln, but I think that is a base canard.) During his career in Washington, he set two records that will likely stand forever; one, he made the cover of Time more times (23, I think) than any photographer before or since; and, two, he knocked over more glasses of Scotch whiskey at Duke Zeibert's bar than any man alive.

In fact, observers on the scene calculate that in 27 years, Wally spilled enough Scotch to float the Queen Mary.

Anyway, he was chummy with my friend Don Steffen, and frequently hunted deer out of Don's cabin near Middletown, VA, within sight of Little North Mountain. And thereby hangs, as they say, the tale.

One cold November day some years ago, Wally, Don and his sons Donnie and Mark, went over to hunt with Wilmer Rosenberger, who lived at the base of Little North Mountain, which is not so little. They worked out a plan and pretty much split up; some of them going all the way to the top spine. Wally took a stand about halfway up and hunkered down beside a big rock, his 30.06 pump gun at the ready.

After a while, Wally heard some shooting up above him and, thumbing the safety off the 30.06, peered keenly up through the hardwoods. Pretty soon, here comes a humungous 10-point buck, pounding hell-for-leather down the mountain about 60 yards away, and he doesn't see or smell Wally for spit. Brother Bennett lets fly with one, but about that time the buck takes a flying leap over a deadfall, and he missed. Damn! But he's got time for one more shot and pulls the slide back...not far enough. The spent shell-casing fails to eject completely, and when he slams the slide forward again, the fresh round becomes horribly jammed. Wally struggles and struggles, to no avail. Then he starts screaming, "SONUVABITCH, SONUVABITCH, SONUVABITCH!" and they hear him all the way to Roanoke.

Meantime, of course, old Mr. Buck is long gone, having a cool drink, by now, in the Shenandoah.

Locals claim that sometimes, even today, on a frosty November morning when the wind is just right, you can still hear the faint cry "sonuvabitch, sonuvabitch, sonuva**bitch**," echoing through the hills over by Little North Mountain.

Fortunately, Wally's a better cook than he is a hunter and he gave me the following recipe for roast goose in a bag. It works equally well with two ducks...wild ones, of course. If you try to cook domestic goose or ducks this way, you end up with a bag full of fat.

WALLY BENNETT'S 2 DUCKS IN A BAG

Wally used to prepare this as his contribution to Don Steffen's annual game dinner. It was always a hit. It works just as well with 1 goose or 2 ducks.

2 ducks or one large goose
½ jar orange marmalade
1 cup bouillon or chicken stock
1 pkg. French's brown gravy mix
1 small can Mandarin orange slices, with juice
1½ tsp. salt
¼ cup flour
1 6 oz. can frozen orange juice, thawed but not diluted
2 oz. Grand Marnier

Mix all ingredients except the birds, and pour into a large oven brown-in bag. Prick the skin of the birds and put in the bag, turning to coat. Close the bag with a twist-um. Put bag in roasting pan. Make 3 or 4 slits in the top of the bag so it doesn't explode all over your oven. Cook in a pre-heated 375 degree oven 2 - 2½ hours for goose, 1 - 1½ hours for ducks.

Skim any excess fat off the gravy, stir and serve.

Wally used to serve this with Scotch. You may prefer rice or noodles, and a green salad, with chilled white wine.

ROAST DUCKS WITH MUSHROOM GRAVY

3 or 4 ducks, well washed
2 or 3 apples, quartered
2 or 3 onions, quartered
2 pinches thyme
flour, pepper, salt, butter, cooking oil

Mix flour, pepper, salt, and thyme in plastic bag. Add ducks and shake to coat. Brown them in butter and a little oil and set aside. Stuff with apple and onion pieces.

Gravy mix

1 can golden mushroom soup
1 can beef broth or bouillon
½ lb. fresh mushrooms, sliced
1 tsp. Worcestershire sauce
1 pinch each, parsley and thyme
¼ cup red wine
salt and pepper

Put the stuffed birds in an oven roasting pan or Dutch oven. Combine the gravy mix ingredients, stir and pour over the birds. Cover and bake 1½ to 2 hours, or until the ducks are tender, basting occasionally.

When the birds are done, remove to a heated serving platter and cut them up. Stir the gravy and pour into a heated gravy boat or bowl.

Oven roasted potatoes and a green vegetable (anything but broccoli) are good choices with this.

Some years ago, when my son Chris was 12, he began to go duck hunting with me. We agreed on two things: first, I would set the decoys and he would call the ducks; second, we would not shoot at ducks outside the set. If we couldn't bring them inside 20 yds., we weren't doing our jobs. Chris took his job seriously, quickly becoming a good caller.

One sunny bluebird day we were in our blind north of Denver, and nothing was flying. Finally, Chris spotted five mallards and began patiently calling. His call turned them, and they were coming straight to the decoys without a pass-by to look us over.

Then the guys in a nearby blind saw them, and rudely began to call—badly. The confused ducks grabbed for some sky, and the other hunters stopped calling. Again Chris patiently began to call. Again the ducks turned to his call and headed in—and again the other callers ruined it. After a third time around, the ducks gave up and headed out of town.

With all the indignation of a 12-year-old foiled by stupid adults, Chris hollered at the other hunters, "Why don't you take that damn duck call out of the BOX?"

Bob Lamson,
Denver, CO

ROAST CURRIED DUCK

2 mallards
2 medium onions, stuck with cloves
1 pinch thyme
1 tbsp. hot curry
4 tbsp. red currant jelly
¼ cup Karo or pancake syrup

Rub ducks with softened butter, sprinkle with pepper, salt and thyme. Put a cloved onion in each cavity. Put ducks in roasting pan or Dutch oven, cover, and bake in a 325 degree oven 1½ to 2 hours, until ducks are tender. Mix the curry, jelly and syrup and baste the birds frequently after the first ¾ of an hour. When done, serve with rice, stir-fried Chinese vegetables and plum wine.

ROAST DUCK WITH SAUERKRAUT

Here's a change of pace from the fruit-based ducks and geese we've been talking about up till now. It will also work well with grouse, partridge, or pheasant. Beer, sauerkraut and caraway seed make the principal difference.

2 mallards or other ducks
2 apples, stuck with cloves
1 lg. can sauerkraut, drained
2 medium onions, sliced thin
2 slices raw bacon, chopped up
1 can beer
2 tsp. caraway seed
butter, pepper, salt

Stuff the birds with cloved apples, rub well with softened butter, sprinkle with pepper and salt. Spread sauerkraut on the bottom of a roasting pan or Dutch oven, cover with sliced onion, chopped bacon, pepper, salt and caraway seed. Place birds on top. Pour in the beer. Cover and roast in a 325 degree oven for 1½ hours or until ducks are tender, basting frequently with melted butter.

Boiled new potatoes in their jackets, a good Jewish rye bread, and lots of cold beer go well with the ducks and sauerkraut.

BARBECUED DUCK

Doug Ensor of Newport News, VA, sent me the following recipe which makes my mouth water just to read it. I've found that it works just as well with rabbits and upland game birds as with ducks.

4 ducks, cleaned and split lengthwise
1 cup salad oil
¼ cup vinegar
¼ cup red wine
1 small onion, minced
1 garlic clove, minced
1 tsp. grated lemon peel
4 tbsp. Worcestershsire sauce
4 tbsp. A-1 sauce
½ cup catsup
¼ tsp. cayenne pepper
1 tsp. celery salt
¼ tsp. black pepper
juice of ½ lemon
several drops of Tabasco

Combine all sauce ingredients and simmer 20 minutes, stirring frequently. Baste ducks generously with sauce and grill over charcoal fire, turning every five minutes and basting heavily each time. The meat should be ready to fall off the bone in 30 - 40 minutes. Serve with corn on the cob, cole slaw, and fresh rolls.

DOWNHEARTED QUAIL

Quail are almost too good to do anything to, except broil with a little pepper and salt and butter. I've had them at Sam Arnold's fine restaurant, The Fort, in the foothills outside of Denver. His chefs flame broil them on the grill, alongside the buffalo and elk steaks, brushing them with melted butter and a little seasoned salt. Fabulous!

GRILLED QUAIL

1 or 2 quail per person
butter, pepper, seasoned salt, paprika

Rub the quail well with softened butter. Season with pepper, seasoned salt and paprika. Broil over the coals on the grill or on a green stick until golden brown all over.

Before cooking the quail, rub some butter on a few baking potatoes, sprinkle with salt, wrap in foil, and place in the hot coals. At the same time, place an ear of un-husked corn that you've soaked in salted water for a couple of hours in the coals. Let the potatoes and corn cook for about ¾ of an hour, or until most of the husk has burnt off the corn. Fish them out of the coals when the quail is done. This makes a great camp meal.

SAUTÉED QUAIL WITH LEMON BUTTER

1 or 2 quail per person
1 stick butter
pepper, seasoned salt, lemon juice, white wine

Season the quail with pepper and seasoned salt. Brown in melted butter over medium heat. Add a couple of thinly sliced shallots, or a half-pound of sliced mushrooms, if you like. Add a jigger of bottled lemon juice, and a couple of jiggers of sherry or white wine. Stir, cover and simmer for about 15 minutes, turning the quail once or twice. Remove quail to a hot platter, cover with pan juices and serve with a little boiled rice, a huge green salad, and a bottle of cold white wine.

Of all the game birds in the world, I think pheasant is the most regal...in flight, or on the table, and is my favorite in either circumstance. Like wild turkey, he can be tough and dry, so moist cooking methods are advised.

ROAST PHEASANT À L'ORANGE

Stock for Gravy

2 cups water
1 cup orange juice
1 can chicken broth or bouillon
2 stalks celery, cut up
2 medium onions, quartered
1 pinch thyme
heart, liver, giblets, pepper, salt, bay leaf

Combine all ingredients, bring to a boil, cover and simmer for 1½ hours. Set aside. Remove organs, chop up for use in stuffing or gravy.

Stuffing

1 box Uncle Ben's Wild and Long grain rice mixture
½ cup orange juice
½ cup chicken broth or chicken bouillon

Follow the directions for stuffing on the box, substitute a half cup of orange juice and half cup of chicken broth for one of the two cups of water called for. Add the chopped up organ meats if you like, or save for the gravy. Stuff the birds lightly, closing the opening with a skewer.

Put the birds in a roasting pan or Dutch oven, with a strip or two of raw bacon placed on top. Season with salt, pepper, and a pinch of thyme. Cover or seal tightly with aluminum foil. Roast in a 325 degree oven for one hour. Test for doneness. If it needs a little more time, uncover and cook until done. Place on a hot serving platter.

Put 2 cups of strained stock in a saucepan, add pan juices, a small can of mandarin orange pieces, or a fresh orange, sliced thin, and a couple of ounces of Grand Marnier. Stir and simmer

for 5 or 6 minutes. Thicken with a little cornstarch and water, or a package of brown gravy mix. Simmer another 3 or 4 minutes, stirring frequently until smooth.

PHEASANT IN SOUR CREAM

2 ringnecks
2 shallots, sliced thin
½ lb. mushrooms, sliced
½ cup red wine
1 pkg. onion soup mix
1 cup sour cream
1 cup chicken broth or bouillon
pepper, salt, thyme

Season the birds with pepper, salt and thyme. Brown them in a half stick of butter in a large skillet or Dutch oven. Mix the shallots, mushrooms, wine, onion soup mix, and chicken broth and pour over the birds. Cover and simmer for one hour, or until birds are done. Remove birds, add sour cream to skillet, stir and simmer for a few minutes. Pour over pheasants, and serve.

The pheasant, a kingly bird, deserves something special to go with it...like oven roasted potatoes, fresh peas with pearl onions, or string beans almandine, hearts of palm salad, and a good bottle of Merlot.

BROILED PARTRIDGE OREGANATO

You'll need about four pounds of birds for this, cut up in serving pieces, and well washed. Soak the birds for about an hour in a mixture of 2/3 water, 1/3 vinegar or red wine, and two tablespoons of salt. Stir and turn them a couple of times. Pat them dry, set aside and proceed as indicated below.

4 lbs. partridge, cut up and soaked
½ cup olive oil
¼ cup red wine
¼ cup lemon juice
1 tsp. parsley flakes
2 tsp. oregano
1 pinch basil
1 clove garlic, minced
pepper and salt

Sprinkle the birds with pepper and salt, and arrange in a broiling pan. Mix the other ingredients in a bowl and brush the birds generously with the mixture. Put the pan five or six inches below the flame and broil for 20 minutes. Turn the pieces, brush again, and broil for another 15 or 20 minutes, until the birds are brown and tender. Keep brushing the mixture on the birds during the broiling process. Heat the remaining mixture and serve as gravy if you like. When done, put on a pre-heated serving platter and serve piping hot. A side order of pasta tossed in olive oil, lots of basil, and some Romano or Parmesan cheese, some crusty Italian bread, and a bottle of Chianti should finish it off well.

FISH

Some cynic has said that fishing is the only activity in the world where you can sit on your fanny under a tree all day and still give the appearance of doing something productive. I know that I have thunk through more than one problem doing just that. Fishing is truly therapeutic.

Though I'm basically a worm-dunker, I know there are thousands of people like my friend Ed Baruth, who would kill for the chance to cast a bit of fluffed up deer hair called a Sparse Gray Hackle, or some such, over a pristine pool in the rushing waters of the Clark's Fork.

Worms or flies, salt water or fresh, fishing is about as much fun as you can have in public, and the catch is worth treating well, whether it's an Oregon salmon, a Jersey shore blue fish, or a Colorado trout.

Here are some recipes for those and other species that I think you'll enjoy.

My son and I were camped alongside the Cimarron near Owl Creek Pass in Colorado's San Juan range, worm-dunking for trout in the nearby Silverjack reservoir. We had a couple of glorious days, plenty of good food and drink, and absolutely buckets of filial comradeship; but not one damn fish.

Our neighbor in the small camp ground walked over late the second day and handed me a string of 6 or 7 of the best looking 1½ to 2 lb. rainbows you ever saw.

"Take these," he said. "I got more than I can eat. Got 'em on worms...deep."

He obviously knew something about trout fishing that had escaped us.

We filleted them, had some for dinner that night with succotash, home fries, and cold Coors, and had the rest for breakfast next morning with scrambled eggs and fresh biscuits.

My son says if you don't know how to fish, it pays to have a friendly neighbor who does. He's grown up to be a smartass.

PAN FRIED TROUT FILLETS

6 trout fillets
1 egg
½ cup milk
1 cup corn meal
pepper, salt, paprika, butter or bacon drippings

Mix egg and milk in a bowl; corn meal, pepper, salt and paprika in a plastic bag. Dip the fillets in the egg mixture, then shake in the bag to coat. Fry in butter or bacon fat over a medium-hot campfire or the ol' Coleman stove. When they are golden brown and crispy, and the meat flakes easily, they are done.

BAKED FILLETS IN CHEDDAR, #1

My sister-in-law Jan sent me this one. It's delicious and easy. It works with trout, blue gill, or any pan fish.

1 lb. fish fillets
2 tbsp. butter
2 tbsp. flour
2 cups milk
½ lb. sharp cheddar cheese, grated
salt and pepper, pinch of dry mustard

Place fish in a shallow baking dish or oven roasting pan. In a saucepan, melt butter, add flour, salt, pepper and mustard. Stir as butter melts. Gradually add milk, stir until just boiling. Stir in cheese, cooking and stirring until the mixture is well blended and smooth. Pour over fish and bake in a 375 degree oven for 20 - 25 minutes.

BAKED FILLETS IN CHEDDAR, #2

This is basically the same idea as #1; but omit the flour and milk. Melt the cheese in 2 cups of beer, add a teaspoon of dry mustard, two good dashes of Worcestershire sauce, and a dash of Tabasco. Stir until cheese is melted, adding more beer if necessary. Bake as in #1.

BAKED STUFFED TROUT

My friend Bill Warnken and his son, Chris, run The Top Gun Sports Center in Kitteridge, CO, and they always seem to know where the deer are, where the fish are running, and what they're biting on. Bill's a competitive shooter, a fisherman of local repute, and a very handy guy with the pots and pans. This is his recipe.

3 slices bacon, diced
2 tbsp. onion, diced
3 cups soft bread crumbs (about 6 slices)
2 tbsp. parsley
½ tsp. grated lemon rind
1 ¼ tsp. salt
1 pinch ground sage
1 egg
6 ready to cook trout (½ lb. each)
½ stick butter
pepper, paprika

Sauté bacon until crisp, remove and drain on paper towels. Stir onion into the drippings and sauté until soft. Pour over bread crumbs, parsley, lemon rind, ¼ tsp. salt, sage and bacon in a bowl. Beat eggs and milk together, pour over bread mixture and toss lightly to mix. Wash trout thoroughly in cold water, pat dry, and place in a single layer in a greased roasting pan or cookie sheet. Mix remaining salt, pepper, and a couple of pinches of paprika. Sprinkle in cavities and over the outside of the trout. Stuff each fish with about 1/3 cup of stuffing. Brush with melted butter. Bake in a 350 degree oven for 25 minutes or until fish flakes easily. Serve on a heated platter, garnished with lemon wedges and fresh parsley. Yes!

STUFFED TROUT IN THE PAN

1 2 lb. trout (or two 1 lb. trout)
1 onion, sliced thin
1 stalk of celery, chopped fine
½ lb. mushrooms, sliced
½ tsp. parsley
1 pinch tarragon
pepper, salt, butter, lemon juice, white wine

Sauté the celery, onion and mushrooms in some butter, seasoning with the salt, pepper, parsley, and tarragon, stirring occasionally until the onion is soft. Spoon the mixture into the cavity of the fish, add a little more butter, and brown the trout lightly on both sides. Add a splash of white wine and a squeeze of lemon juice, cover, and simmer for another 5 minutes or so until the fish flakes off easily to the fork.

Last time we had this we served it with fresh asparagus, a green salad with red onions and gorgonzola dressing, and a cold bottle of cabernet blanc. It was *very* good.

BEER BATTER CATFISH

We're going to call it catfish, but you can do this with damn near anything that swims, from crappies to store-bought shrimp. I tended bar in a restaurant once, where the chef would only use Killian's Irish Red beer in the batter; but I suppose you can use anything from stout or pale ale to Miller Light.

½ stick of butter
1 cup Bisquick
1 egg
¾ cup your favorite beer
pepper, salt, pinch of dry mustard
catfish fillets

Melt butter in skillet over medium heat. Mix Bisquick, egg, beer, pepper, salt and mustard in bowl. Add more beer if it's too thick, or flour if too thin. Dip fillets in the mixture to coat thoroughly on both sides. Fry until golden brown. Hush puppies go well with this, or hot biscuits with honey, cole slaw and, of course, buckets of cold beer...what else?

POACHED SALMON VIN BLANC

Whole or filleted salmon, trout, or bass; indeed, almost any fish small enough to fit in a decent-sized skillet can be poached to good advantage, light and delicious.

> 4 - 6 pieces of fish, whole or filleted
> 2 tbsp. butter
> ½ cup white wine
> 2 shallots or 1 medium onion, sliced very thin
> 1 bay leaf
> 3 or 4 thin slices of fresh lemon
> pepper, salt, pinch of dill weed or tarragon

Melt butter in skillet over medium heat. Add fish, scatter shallots over the top. Add lemon slices, wine and seasonings. Cover, reduce heat, and simmer for 10 or 15 minutes, or until fish flakes easily with a fork.

Serve with boiled parslied potatoes, buttered carrots, and chilled white wine.

BASIC BROILED FISH

Broiling is probably the simplest method of cooking any fish, whether it's a whole cutthroat, a half-dozen little pan fish, or a thick salmon, shark, tuna, or halibut steak. A bit of butter, some pepper and salt and a pinch of parsley enhance rather than disguise the natural flavor of the fish.

For oven broiling, line a roasting pan with aluminum foil and smear a little melted butter or light cooking oil over the surface...just enough to keep the fish from sticking. If you put in too much, the oil or butter will burn under the broiler and smoke up your kitchen. Add the fish, dot with butter, season and broil about 4 inches from the flame 6 to 8 minutes. Turn with a spatula and repeat on the other side. Squeeze a bit of fresh lemon juice over the top and serve.

For broiling on a grill or campfire you might consider investing in one of those hinged wire arrangements where you clamp the fish lightly between the two halves of this gadget, turning the whole thing by the long handles, rather than trying to scrape charred fish off the grill with a pancake turner. Otherwise put a sheet of heavy-duty aluminum foil on the grill and proceed as with oven broiling.

Try not to turn your salmon or other steak fish more than once as they fall apart easily.

BARBECUED SNAPPER ON THE GRILL

Captain John Quigley and I were heading out of Barnegat Inlet on the south Jersey shore for a day of fluke fishing along the sandy beaches of Long Beach Island. The big blues had abandoned the shore line a few days previously, and were schooling up nearly 20 miles out toward England; a long trip in a 17-ft. Boston Whaler. So, what the hay. A day of bottom fishing and a cooler full of beer and sandwiches didn't seem like a bad idea.

But, as we cleared the end of the jetty, Cap'n John's steely gaze picked up the sight of a flock of gulls working over a submerged sand bar about a half-mile up the beach. He spun the wheel hard to port, shoved the throttle home and we pounded north, just outside the surf.

"Better re-rig for spin casting with hammered lures, Pied," he said. John always called me the Pied Piper because of my natural affinity for small children.

In about 10 minutes we were over the bar in less than a dozen feet of water. A huge school of snapper—baby blue fish—were chasing killies and spearing and other little bait fish up to the surface, and were fighting the screaming, diving gulls for them. It was an absolute feeding frenzy. Fish were jumping all over the place, the gulls were wheeling and diving all around us, making a hell of a racket. We boated a fish with every cast and foul-hooked three gulls. In the 20 minutes or so that this mad scene lasted we took 107 snappers, ranging from ¾ to 1½ pounds.

It ended as suddenly as it began. The blues and gulls disappeared and we headed back in, the little Boston Whaler almost up to her gunnels in flopping snappers. I had never seen anything like it. It took us several hours to fillet all those little puppies, and we froze over 50 two-pound bags of them.

We put about 5 lbs. of them into big pans of home-made barbecue sauce for a couple of hours, invited some neighbors over, drank some beer, and cooked them right on the grill. They were light, tender, and perfect with the french fries, cole slaw and iced beer we had with them.

BAKED, STUFFED BLUEFISH

1 3 - 4 lb. bluefish
½ cup seasoned bread crumbs
¼ cup grated Parmesan cheese
1 stalk celery, cut up fine
1 medium onion, sliced thin
¼ lb. mushrooms, sliced
6 black olives, sliced
6 green olives, sliced
1 can crushed tomatoes
1 pinch thyme
1 pinch basil
pepper, salt, olive oil

Remove head and tail, wash and scale fish. Cut off most of the dark belly meat, which imparts a strong, oily and fishy flavor. Sauté onion, celery, mushrooms and spices in a little olive oil or butter. Drain excess oil. In a bowl, mix sauté with seasoned bread crumbs and grated cheese. Put fish in a roasting pan lined with aluminum foil, open it as wide as you can. Spread a layer of crushed tomatoes the length of the cavity. Spread the sautéed mixture as the next layer. Put a few thin slices of onion and the sliced olives on top, alternating by color. Close the fish as well as you can, holding it together with toothpicks. Seal pan with aluminum foil and place in a 350 degree oven. Bake 20 minutes or until fish flakes easily.

This recipe works as well with striped bass, sea bass, or young king mackerel.

SOFT SHELL CRABS

Obviously, soft shell crabs are not a game species, but if you are water-fowling or sport fishing in the tidal estuaries from Cape Cod to the Virginia capes, and these beauties are available, it would be a shame not to enjoy them for supper one night. Depending on their size, you'll probably need 3 for each person, and though they are expensive as hell, they're definitely worth a financial splurge.

Pan Fried

Clean, wash, and pat dry the crabs. Dredge with flour, pepper, salt, and a pinch of thyme. Be careful; without it's hard shell, there's not much holding that crab together but willpower, and the legs and feelers break off easily. Fry in butter until golden brown on both sides. Serve with tartar sauce and lemon wedges, french fries and cole slaw.

Batter Fried

On page 116, there's a recipe for Beer Batter Catfish. Make your batter according to that recipe, omitting the dry mustard, and adding a few dashes of paprika. Coat the crabs with the batter, and fry until golden brown. With a little catsup or tartar sauce, these make great sandwiches on soft kaiser rolls, or between slabs of buttered sourdough bread.

Sautéed

Melt a half stick of butter in a skillet over medium heat. Add the crabs, salt, pepper, and a pinch of parsley. Brown lightly on both sides. Add a squeeze of fresh lemon juice and an ounce or two of white wine. Reduce heat, cover and simmer for 8 - 10 minutes. Do not over-cook (which can be said for *all* fish).

Serve with buttered boiled potatoes, fresh kale, slabs of sourdough toast, and chilled white wine.

SEAFOOD GUMBO

A hunter friend claims that if you get lost in the woods, the best thing to do is pull a bottle of gin and a bottle of vermouth out of your pack, and make yourself a martini. As soon as you get the proportions to your liking, some sonuvabitch will jump out of the woods and declare, "That's no way to make a martini," and then you won't be lost anymore, or anyway not alone.

Similarly, there are strongly-held opinions on how to make a "real" gumbo...all of them different. Even cajuns disagree on whether you must use the powdered sassafras called gumbo filé, or whether you pronounce it file or fee-lay. Most agree that you must begin by making a roux (roo), a mixture of flour, butter and essence, and that you must have okra.

However you make it, gumbo and rice is a zesty, hearty meal for camp or kitchen.

At risk of starting an argument, here's a "simple" gumbo recipe that works with shrimp, cut up pieces of fish, or both.

Use a large pot or Dutch oven

2 lbs. raw shrimp, veined
2 lbs. raw fish, boned, skinned and cut in chunks
¼ cup chopped celery
3 large onions, chopped
2 bunches scallions, including green ends, chopped
3 garlic cloves, minced
1 jar Paul Newman's Sockaroonie marinara sauce
2 tbsp. chopped, fresh parsley
2 cups okra, fresh or frozen
1 or 2 bay leaves
1 tbsp. gumbo filé
1/3 cup flour
1 stick butter
thyme, salt, black and red (cayenne) pepper, Tabasco sauce, lemon juice, water or chicken broth.

Put the flour and butter in a Dutch oven over medium heat. Stir and cook until well blended and turning brown. Add filé and continue stirring. Add garlic, onions, scallions, celery, parsley and okra, stirring until well mixed, adding a little water or chicken broth as necessary to moisten. Add salt, black and red pepper (about a teaspoon each), a squeeze of fresh lemon, and 4 or 5 shakes of Tabasco. Stir and simmer for about 10 minutes. Add fish, shrimp and marinara sauce and simmer another 5 minutes, thinning if necessary with chicken broth or water. It should be fairly thick. Remove from heat when fish and shrimp are tender. (Sample a little.) Ladle over boiled white rice and serve with soda crackers and lots of cold beer.

BARBECUED SHARK STEAK

I don't suppose any of us is going to catch a shark any time soon. But if you're hunting or fishing anywhere near either coast, shark steaks are available in most supermarkets, and make a hearty, satisfying meal. Tuna, scrod, or haddock will also do nicely.

Rub the steaks on both sides with a little lemon juice and a dash or two of Tabasco sauce. Brush with a good, spicy bottled barbecue sauce, or your own, homemade version. Oven broil, or do them on the grill, for about 6 minutes per side.

On a cold day such things as hot baked potatoes,
all sprinkled over with fresh-ground pepper and sweet butter,
or creamy tomato soup with a faint smell of cinnamon to it,
or a rare, steaming beef, pink and succulent;
these are the things that flow first into our remembrance on cold days.

M.F.K. Fisher
The Art of Eating

STEWS, SOUPS AND CHOWDERS

If you've ever frozen your buns off sitting on a deer stand, the wind howling and the snow blowing in your face, or sat in a duck blind, the icy rain unerringly finding the only unpatched tear in your slicker and running down your back, you know there are only a couple of things the mere thought of which will bring you a flash of instant warmth.

First, of course, is the thought of about three fingers of sour mash! Right behind that for many of us is the vision of a big pot of steaming venison stew all bubbly and thick with maybe a couple of dumplings floating in it; or a creamy oyster stew with paprika; or Mrs. Fisher's home-made tomato soup, hot and rich and smelling faintly of cinnamon.

So many of the critters we hunt and fish lend themselves to stewing, that an entire cook book could easily be devoted to just game and fish stews and soups. The ones we've gathered here are fairly representative and all are good. You may find one or two that become your favorites.

Stews need long, slow cooking to allow the flavors to blend and to fill your camp or kitchen with their wonderful aromas. And if you haven't got or don't care for one or more of the listed ingredients, don't worry about it. Omit or substitute; improvise. Stews and soups are pretty forgiving.

Recipes are grouped as follows:

Meat, big game and small;
Birds, upland and water fowl;
Fish and seafood.

SAVORY VENISON STEW

3 lbs. deer, elk or moose meat, cut in bite-sized chunks
2 cups beer
2 cups water
2 pinches thyme
1 bay leaf
2 onions, cut up
4 or 5 potatoes, cut up
4 or 5 carrots, cut up
1 garlic clove, minced
1 tbsp. Worcestershire sauce
1 tbsp. vinegar
pepper, salt, flour, butter

Put about 1/3 cup flour in a plastic bag, add pepper and salt, shake to mix. Add meat and shake to coat. Brown the meat in butter and a little cooking oil in a Dutch oven. Add the rest of the ingredients and stir to mix. (You can add a can of tomatoes, and a package of frozen peas or lima beans if you like.) Bring to a boil, cover, reduce heat and simmer slowly for about 2 hours. Check after 1½ hours to adjust spices, adding more pepper and salt. Stir in a little flour and water mix if necessary to thicken. This is also about the right time to add dumplings. Check the recipe on the Bisquick box and proceed accordingly.

VENISON STEW WITH BURGUNDY

3 lb. deer, elk, moose or antelope, cut in bite-size pieces
2 cups beef broth
1 cup burgundy or other dry red wine
1 pkg. onion soup mix
3 or 4 potatoes, cut up
3 or 4 carrots, cut up
¾ lb. pearl onions, peeled but whole
2 garlic cloves, peeled but whole
1 pinch basil
1 pinch thyme
½ lb. mushrooms, sliced
2 tbsp. Worcestershire sauce
1 tbsp. vinegar
10 - 12 juniper berries
flour, butter, pepper and salt, paprika

Mix 1/3 cup flour, pepper, salt and paprika in a bag. Add venison and shake to coat. Save the seasoned flour; you can use it later to thicken the stew if you like. Brown the meat in butter in a Dutch oven. Add the rest of the ingredients except the mushrooms. Stick toothpicks in the garlic cloves so you can find them and fish them out before serving. If you don't have juniper berries, add a couple of tablespoons of red currant jelly at this point. Adjust seasonings adding pepper and salt to taste. If you want more liquid, add water or beef broth. Thicken if necessary with dredging flour and a little water, stirring all the while. Add mushrooms. Cover and simmer another 30 minutes.

Hot biscuits or garlic bread and a jug of decent burgundy finish this off beautifully.

VENISON AND KIDNEY STEW

Use the preceding recipe for Venison Stew with Burgundy, adding cut up venison kidneys to the meat. Wash the kidneys thoroughly, cutting away any silverskin and fat. Soak the pieces in salted water for about an hour, drain and pat dry, and brown with the venison chunks.

VENISON STEW PAPRIGASH

3 lbs. cubed venison
2 cups beef broth
1 cup red wine
2 or 3 onions, cut up
2 garlic cloves, minced
2 cans cooked whole tomatoes
1 tbsp. Worcestershire sauce
2 cups sour cream or buttermilk
1 tbsp. paprika
1 pinch basil
pepper and salt, flour, butter

Mix 1/3 cup flour, pepper and salt in a plastic bag. Shake to mix. Add meat and shake to coat. Brown meat in butter in a Dutch oven. Add all ingredients except sour cream. Stir, cover and simmer 1½ hours. Add sour cream, mix, cover and simmer for another half hour. Serve with buttered egg noodles and cold beer.

STEWED RABBIT WITH SHERRY

2 rabbits, cut up
2 cups chicken broth, stock, or bouillon
½ cup dry sherry or white wine
1 lg. can cooked whole tomatoes
2 onions, cut up
5 potatoes, cut up
6 carrots, cut up
1 pinch thyme
1 pinch parsley
1 or 2 bay leaves
1 garlic clove, minced
1 cup sour cream or buttermilk
flour, pepper and salt, butter

Mix 1/3 cup flour, pepper and salt in a bag. Add rabbit and shake to coat. Brown rabbit in butter in Dutch oven. Add all other ingredients except sour cream. Pepper and salt to taste. Cover and simmer about 1 hour. Stir in sour cream, adjust spices, cover and simmer another half hour.

BRUNSWICK STEW

Traditionally a squirrel dish, it works well with rabbit or a mixture of both meats. Use any combination of whatever you've been lucky enough to bag.

    4 squirrels, cut up
    1 lg. pkg. frozen mixed vegetables
    1 pkg. frozen okra
    4 or 5 potatoes, cut up
    5 cups chicken broth or bouillon
    1 lg. can whole cooked tomatoes
    2 onions, cut up
    1 garlic clove, minced
    ½ tsp. thyme
    flour, salt, pepper, butter or bacon fat, Tabasco sauce

Mix flour, pepper, salt in a bag. Add squirrel pieces and shake to coat. Brown meat in a Dutch oven in some butter or bacon grease. Add the rest of the ingredients and about 5 or 6 dashes of Tabasco. Pepper and salt to taste. Cover and simmer about 1 hour, or until meat is tender and potatoes are cooked.

If you prefer this stew without the bones, just simmer the meat in the broth or bouillon until it's tender. Remove the meat from the bones and put back in the pot. Then add the rest of the ingredients and proceed as above.

BEAN AND BARLEY SOUP WITH DEER HOCKS

This is a great soup to make early in the hunt to keep on the back of the stove so your camp-mates can ladle out a cup as the spirit moves them. If you don't have deer hocks in the freezer, three or four smoked ham hocks will work. It isn't really necessary to soak the beans overnight. This soup cooks for hours, or maybe days, and the beans get mushy enough.

4 deer hocks
1 pkg. dried navy or white beans
1 cup barley
5 cups water
1 cup white wine
4 onions, cut up
½ cup molasses
2 cloves garlic, minced
2 bay leaves
1 tsp. pepper and salt
1 tbsp. dry mustard
1 pinch each, thyme, basil

Put all ingredients in a Dutch oven, stir, bring to a boil. Skim off suds and gunk. Cover and simmer 2 to 3 hours, until beans are tender. Take the hocks out, remove the bones, cut the meat up into small pieces and put back in the pot. Adjust seasonings and simmer another half hour or so.

You can use black beans, or 3-bean mixture if you like, instead of the navy beans.

Note: A couple of teaspoons of Angostura after a meal like this reduces flatulence, which can be a social factor if four or five of you are sleeping in a small tent or camper.

RABBIT NOODLE SOUP

As is the case with many recipes, this one will also work with any of the upland game birds. Just start out with about 3 lbs. of cleaned, dressed meat, cut up.

3 lbs. rabbit (2 rabbits should do)
6 cups chicken broth or bouillon
2 medium onions, sliced thin
2 stalks celery, cut up
2 carrots, sliced
½ pkg. broad egg noodles
butter, pepper, salt, parsley

Season rabbit pieces with pepper and salt, and brown lightly in hot butter in a Dutch oven. Add all ingredients except noodles. Add pepper and salt to taste, cover and simmer about 45 minutes. Add noodles, bring to a boil, reduce heat and simmer another 10 or 15 minutes until noodles are tender.

CHINESE DUCK SOUP

If you have left over roast duck or goose, pick all the meat from the carcass and cut it into small pieces. Otherwise, simmer a duck in 6 cups of water, a stalk of celery, an onion, a carrot, and some pepper and salt for about 45 minutes. Remove the duck to cool, and strain the stock. Cut the duck into small pieces, and proceed as follows:

- 2 cups cooked duck meat
- 5 - 6 cups chicken broth, stock, or bouillon
- 1 small onion, sliced paper thin
- 5 or 6 scallions, sliced, including most of the green part
- 1 pinch ground ginger
- 1 egg, lightly beaten
- 2 dashes soy sauce
- salt and pepper to taste

Put all ingredients except the beaten egg into a sauce pan and bring to a boil. Using the back of a spoon, force the beaten egg through a strainer into the boiling soup, breaking it up and stirring as it goes into the pot until it solidifies into small shreds. Simmer 10 minutes. Serve with boiled rice or low mein noodles.

SPLIT PEA SOUP WITH HAM HOCKS

Unless you shot the pig, this doesn't qualify as a game recipe, and if you want to be stuffy about it, pass it up. But it's such a damn good soup in a deer camp, I feel it's worth putting in the book.

- 4 or 5 thick cut smoked ham hocks
- 1 pkg. dried split peas
- 2 medium onions, chopped
- 1 carrot, chopped
- 1 potato, diced fine
- 1 clove garlic, minced
- 5 or 6 cups water
- 1 pinch thyme
- 1 tsp. pepper
- ½ tsp. salt

Wash the peas under cold water to remove gunk, then put in a large pot or Dutch oven. Add all other ingredients, stir, cover and simmer for two hours. Remove hocks. When cool enough to handle, remove meat from bones and cut up into small pieces. Pulverize the soup with a potato masher or ricer, or a whisk. If it has gotten too thick, add a little more water. But it should be fairly thick. Add meat, stir and simmer a little longer, particularly if you have added water.

Pour into a heated serving bowl or tureen, sprinkle with croutons, and serve. Yum!

JAMAICAN FISH SOUP

Whether you use small-mouth bass or deep sea bass, it makes a mouth-watering soup. This recipe is so easy I will probably get arrested for charging money for it.

1 lb. fresh fish fillets, cut in chunks
6 cups chicken broth or bouillon
2 onions, sliced very thin
1 pinch allspice
1 pinch ground ginger
1 pinch cayenne pepper
1 tsp. salt

Combine all ingredients in soup pot. Bring to a boil, reduce heat, cover and simmer 15 - 20 minutes, or until fish flakes easily. This tangy soup should bite just a little. Add a dash of Tabasco to your bowl if you like it hotter. To make it a bit more substantial, add a half cup of uncooked white rice when combining all the ingredients, and simmer till rice is done.

FISH CHOWDER

1 lb. fresh fillets, cut in pieces
½ lb. raw bacon, diced
1 large onion, chopped
2 stalks celery, chopped
1 lg. can creamed corn
1 lg. bag frozen mixed vegetables for stew
1 quart milk
2 tbsp. flour
pepper, salt, paprika

Cook bacon in Dutch oven until crisp, drain off most of the fat and sauté the onion and celery in the remainder. Add vegetables, milk, fish, pepper, salt and paprika. Stir, bring to a boil, cover and simmer until vegetables are done, about 10 - 12 minutes.

MANHATTAN CLAM CHOWDER

2 doz. large chowder clams or two 10-oz. cans minced clams with the juice
½ lb. bacon, diced
2 onions, chopped
2 stalks celery, chopped
1 lg. pkg. frozen mixed vegetables
1 lg. can stewed tomatoes
6 cups water
1 tsp. each pepper and salt
2 tsp. thyme

Wash and open the clams. Preserving as much of the juice as possible, run them through an old fashioned meat grinder, or chop them up by hand. Put them in a mixing bowl and set aside. Sauté bacon, onions and celery with a little pepper and salt. Drain on a paper towel. Mix all ingredients in a large soup pot or Dutch oven. Bring to a boil, reduce heat, cover and simmer for 1 hour.

Everything anybody ever wanted to know about oysters, including the fact that they "R" in season 12 months a year, can be found in M.F.K. Fisher's witty and knowledgeable treatise, *Consider the Oyster*. There are all kinds of recipes in there for oysters: soups, stews, bisques, broiled, baked, fried, and something called a Hang Town Fry, which is like an oyster omelet.

Anyway, I'm not going to try to compete with The Champ, but the following recipe is one that I like, and it goes well on a cool night. It's pretty close to the way it is served in New York at the Oyster Bar in Grand Central Station.

OYSTER STEW

1 qt. oysters, in their liquor
2 cups milk, half and half, or heavy cream
½ stick butter
pepper, celery salt, Worcestershire sauce, paprika

Put the oysters and liquor in a saucepan over medium heat, stir frequently as the oysters heat up and begin to bubble. Add the milk or cream and half the butter. Stir in the pepper, celery salt, and a dash or two of Worcestershire sauce. Continue stirring so the milk doesn't stick. As the oysters begin to fatten up and the edges start to curl, add the other half of the butter and a couple of shakes of paprika. Stir again, and serve piping hot.

STOCK

Stock is the basis for stews, soups, gravies, sauces and some marinades. It is the essence—sometimes highly concentrated—of the flavor of the animal, bird or fish that it comes from. With stock on hand, you eliminate the need for canned chicken or beef broth, or bouillon cubes. It's easy to make and stores well in tightly sealed quart (or bigger) jars or milk containers in the fridge.

Venison Stock

Bones, lots of bones; knuckles, ribs, whatever, of deer, elk, etc. Whack them up with an axe so they fit in a pot, remove all fat, but don't worry about bits of meat clinging to them.

2 onions, quartered
2 carrots, quartered
2 stalks of celery, halved, including leaves
1 cup red wine
2 bay leaves
2 garlic cloves, minced
1 tsp. each, salt, pepper, thyme, basil
water to cover.

Put all ingredients in a large pot and bring to a boil. Let it boil, skim off any gunk that rises to the top and reduce heat. Cover and simmer for 1½ hours or so. If you want a reduced and stronger-flavored result, remove cover and simmer another half hour. Throw out the bones, strain the stock through a fine strainer or a hunk of cheesecloth. Cool and refrigerate.

Wild Bird Stock

When preparing your grouse, goose, mallards or pat for table, save the necks, hearts, livers and giblets. After you've roasted or otherwise cooked and eaten the birds, use the carcass and bones for stock, adding the necks, hearts, livers and giblets.

    2 onions, quartered
    2 carrots, quartered
    2 stalks celery, halved, with leaves
    1 cup white wine
    2 bay leaves
    1 tsp. each, pepper, salt, parsley, thyme, sage
    water to cover

Proceed as for venison stock.

Fish Stock

After you've filleted your trout, bass or blue fish, eviscerate them and throw what's left into the stock pot. Some people don't even bother to gut them, but I have a problem with that. But heads, tails, bones...throw them in the pot and proceed as above, omitting the sage.

It was cold, getting dark, and there was about a foot of snow on the ground. Jim Brown and I had spent a fruitless day in search of game, but it had been snowing and blowing and the deer were down in the swamps or up on the ridges, or some damn place, hunkered down and waiting it out. Jim walked about thirty yards away from my new Oldsmobile station wagon, and began jacking the shells out of his .35 Remington lever-action Marlin. He lost half of them in the snow, and the ones he could find were wet when he put them in his pocket.

I was hunting with a brand new Remington 700, with 5 rounds of 180-grain 30.06 in it. I had put 25 rounds through it to sight in, but that's all it had ever been fired. I unlocked the tailgate on the wagon, swung it open, and began ejecting the shells into the back of the car, not wanting to lose them in the snow. The round in the chamber ejected cleanly, but when I slammed the bolt home on the second round...BLAM! That son of a bitch went off with a roar that I still dream about.

The muzzle of the rifle was in the car at the time. I dimly heard Jim giving me a lot of sunuvabitch and goddam, as I looked for the bullet hole. There wasn't much of a one in the upholstered side panel in the back of the wagon. Still in a dazed kind of shock that follows the accidental discharge of a firearm, I went around to see what damage the bullet had done on the way out.

God in Heaven! There was a 5-pointed star burst about the size of a grapefruit in that left rear quarter panel and liquid was pouring from somewhere inside the hole in to the snow. Christ, I thought, I've shot the goddam gas tank, and we won't get off this friggin mountain till spring!

As I bent down to get an identifying sniff, Jim said, "Don't bother, idiot. Don't you know scotch when you smell it? Not only have you shot a helluva hole in your brand new station wagon, you have also murdered a perfectly defenseless half-gallon of Ballantines. Keeerist!" Sure enough, the round had gone through a small storage locker built into the rear of the wagon. All that was left of a half-gallon of scotch and a half-gallon of vodka was millions of tiny shards of glass.

I was shaking. I'd never had a weapon go off by accident before, and was at a loss to explain how it happened. We wound our way down the narrow, twisting roads. It was full dark now, and the snow was getting heavier. Half an hour later, we pulled into the parking lot at the Antrim Lodge, where we were staying that season. The town of Roscoe was decorated for the approaching Christmas season and it looked pretty in the snow.

We went to our respective rooms to change for dinner, and I lay the rifle gingerly in the corner, having long since unloaded the rest of the shells out the bottom, which I should have done in the first place. We met at the bar in the big tap room for a couple of badly-needed drinks. Just as we sat down for dinner at a table near the huge fireplace, we were joined by Dick Sergeant, a New York City homicide detective who was going to hunt with us for the next couple of days.

After hellos and some general chit-chat, Dick looked me square in the eye and I sensed the gentle kick he gave Jim under the table as he said, "Gee, Jimmy, I spotted your new wagon out in the lot," (it was the only car there with Virginia plates, which didn't take a helluva lot of detective work to figure out,) "and I thought, Wow, some bastard shot a hole in Jim's new car.

"Then I realized, being a detective and all, that what I saw was an exit hole, not an entry hole, and not seeing any signs of forced entry, I really wonder how the sonuvabitch got in there to shoot your car from the inside. Have you called the state troopers yet?" He delivered all this with a straight face, which is more than I can say for Jim Brown, who was nearly strangling trying to keep from laughing.

"What are you, Sam Spade? Nick Charles? Did you come up here to hunt or to play Nosey Parker? Detective! You couldn't detect your way out of the men's room. Why don't you order a drink or something and mind your business." I retreated into a silent funk as the two of them ribbed me unmercifully all night.

But we bagged a couple of deer, and I dropped Jim off in Jackson Heights and headed back to Virginia where I had to tell my wife that I shot the new car and I don't even want to discuss that part of it. But the cruelest barb of all came when I called the insurance company to see if my comprehensive covered bullet damage.

"Nationwide is on your side. How can I help you?"

"This is Mr. Hayes, policy # so and so. I was deer hunting and accidentally shot my car and I want to know, etc. etc."

"Gasp...You shot your car?" (Muffled—"Helen, I got this guy on the phone says he was deer hunting and he shot his car! Did he what? Ha, ha...I'll ask him.")

"Did you think it had horns, Mr. Hayes?" (Dissolve into uncontrollable laughter.)

"!!&%*$#"

When I called Jim Brown to read him this story, we had a good laugh over it. He's now 80 and hasn't hunted in years. In fact, not since this particular incident. He still claims that he quit hunting on orders from his doctor...that his blood pressure was way up and slogging around the mountains in the snow was not good for him, and that it didn't have anything to do with me and any real or perceived carelessness on my part. Come to think of it, having that 30.06 go off in his ear probably didn't do his blood pressure any good at that.

About the gun. A gunsmith later told me all the retaining and adjusting screws on the trigger mechanism were so loose they were falling out, and the thing could have gone off just about whenever it felt like it. But it was still a dumb thing to do.

INNARDS, VARIETY MEATS AND MISCELLANEOUS STUFF

There are lots of folks who go green around the gills at the thought of eating the interior organs of an animal. Yet many a hunter has broiled the still warm liver of his downed deer over a hastily built fire, while continuing to dress him out.

Here are a few recipes for liver and heart, one for kidneys, a couple of somewhat unconventional items, and two for camp bread which didn't seem to fit anyplace else.

VENISON LIVER WITH BACON AND ONIONS

1 deer or elk liver, sliced
½ lb. bacon
2 onions, sliced
flour, pepper, salt

Fry the bacon in a large skillet until crisp. Remove from pan to paper towels to drain. Mix flour, pepper and salt in a bag. Slice the liver into 1 - 2 in. pieces, removing any connective tissue or exterior fat. Shake in the flour mixture to coat. Sauté the onions in the bacon fat until almost soft, add the liver slices. Add pepper and salt to taste, and fry over medium heat until done medium rare, turning once. Remove to hot platter, add crisp bacon slices, and serve with cottage fries.

LIVER AND ONION SAUTÉ

6 - 8 slices fresh venison liver
2 cups beef broth, stock, or bouillon
1 cup dry red wine
2 medium onions, sliced
½ lb. mushrooms, sliced
flour, pepper, salt

Flour and season liver. Brown in melted butter in a skillet. When cooked medium rare, remove to pre-heated platter. Sauté onions and mushrooms in the same skillet. Add stock and wine. Stir. Put liver back in, cover with pan juice and simmer for 10 minutes. Remove liver to heated serving platter. Thicken the pan juice with a little corn starch or flour and water. Pour over liver and serve.

CHARCOAL GRILLED LIVER

6 - 8 slices fresh venison liver
½ stick melted butter
pepper, salt, lemon juice

Mix the butter, pepper and salt, and the juice of half a lemon. Coat the liver with the lemon-butter and grill for about 3 minutes per side.

QUICK BRAISED VENISON HEART

1 deer or elk heart
½ pkg. onion soup mix
½ cup water or beef broth
1/3 cup red wine
flour, pepper, salt, Worcestershire sauce, butter

Slice the heart crossways, in ½ inch slices. Remove any fat, connective tissue, arteries, etc. Coat with flour, pepper and salt, and brown in skillet in melted butter. Add remaining ingredients, including a dash or two of Worcestershire sauce. Stir to mix, cover, and simmer 15 - 20 minutes, or until tender.

BRAISED VENISON KIDNEY

1 deer or elk kidney, sliced or cut in pieces
½ cup beef stock or broth
¼ cup red wine
flour, pepper, salt, butter, paprika, brandy or Cognac

Flour the kidney and season with pepper, salt and paprika.

Cook in a medium hot skillet in melted butter until browned. Add the stock, wine, and a splash of Cognac. Cover and simmer for about 15 minutes. Serve with toast points

BUCK HAVEN VENISON PATÉ

Jack Lamson, owner of the Buck Haven Deer Camp near Burlington, VT, sends this recipe, courtesy of E.J. Little, the camp chef.

½ of a fresh venison liver
1 garlic clove, left whole
2 tsp. chopped parsley
2 pinches thyme
1 pinch basil
1 pinch oregano
1 pinch rosemary
¼ cup water
¼ cup red wine
1 beef bouillon cube
4 slices bacon, cooked and crumbled
3 tbsp. mayonnaise
3 cups Bisquick
1 cup milk
salt and pepper to taste

Soak a half deer liver in salt water for 30 minutes. Cut in ½ in. slices and place in a sauce pan. Add the herbs, spices, garlic, wine, water, bouillon cube, salt and pepper, and cook for 35 to 40 minutes.

Strain, saving the liquid. Combine contents of strainer (liver and spices) with bacon and mayonnaise in blender and process until smooth. Mix Bisquick and milk.

Line the bottom and sides of a greased bread pan with Bisquick dough. Add the liver mixture. Mix 4 tsp. of the liquid saved from cooking with remaining dough and cover the top of the mixture. Bake 15 minutes, or until brown, in a pre-heated 400 degree oven.

Allow to cool, remove from pan, garnish with parsley, and serve in slices.

BOILED MOOSE NOSE

My friend Kay Kerr from Houston, TX, sent me the following narrative recipe, which I pass along without editorial comment.

"...the nose must be cooked for at least an hour or so complete with hide and hair. Cool the nose till you can skin the hide off it easily, and wash thoroughly with cold water. Return to a pot of cold water to cover. Add salt, pepper, and a few bay leaves and boil until tender. Remove and chill. Serve chilled on toast points or crackers."

I am not really sure that Kay is my friend!

COLD TONGUE

Cold sliced tongue makes a great sandwich on fresh rye bread with mustard, mayo or relish, and is worth the effort involved in removing it from the animal. Once removed, put it in a pot, roots and all, cover with water and boil for about an hour. Remove to cool. Cut off roots, fat, etc., and peel.

Put the peeled tongue in a pot and cover with a mixture of 1/3 water, 1/3 vinegar, and 1/3 red wine. Add a sliced onion, a couple of bay leaves, some whole pepper corns, 3 or 4 teaspoons of salt, a few whole cloves and half a dozen juniper berries. Bring to a boil, reduce heat, cover and simmer until the tongue is tender...anywhere from an hour to four hours, depending on the size of the animal. When done, chill it in the pickling mixture overnight. Slice thin and serve with sandwich makings.

JALAPEÑO CORN BREAD

This is what you call your basic sinus-clearer-upper. Whether you serve it hot or cold, it's still hot, and it goes well with a cup of chili. Two or three days old, it makes the basis of a pretty good stuffing for a goose or gobbler.

- 2 cups yellow corn meal
- 2 cups canned creamed corn
- ½ lb. sharp cheddar cheese, grated
- 1 stick butter, melted
- 1 cup milk or buttermilk
- ½ cup canned, drained, chopped jalapeño peppers
- 4 eggs, beaten
- 2 tbsp. baking soda

Combine the corn meal, corn and grated cheese in a bowl and stir until blended. Add the melted butter, milk, peppers, eggs, baking soda, and a pinch of salt. Mix thoroughly. Pour batter into two 7½-inch square greased baking pans, about half and half. Bake in a pre-heated 375 degree oven 45 - 50 minutes, or until done.

BILL WARNKEN'S BEER BREAD

- 3 cups self-rising flour
- 3 tsp. sugar
- 1 can warm beer

Mix all ingredients and put into a well-greased bread pan. Bake at 375 degrees for 1 hour. Sprinkle course salt on top and spread thickly with butter. Return to oven for 5 minutes or so.

Cool and slice.

Bill says in a pinch, you can make this over the campfire, putting your mixture in an old, well-greased coffee can and sticking it right on the grill. Bill is a veteran, and veterans don't lie.

SOME TIPS ON LEFTOVERS

It has been my experience that 5 or 6 hungry hunters pretty well finish up most meals. There is something about being out of doors all day, slogging around in the snow, climbing mountains, or chasing game through the swamps that produces healthy, if not ravenous, appetites.

If you do have anything left over, what do you do with it? Clean the meat or fish from the bones, put it in sealable plastic bags—which take less room than plastic tubs—and re-refrigerate it. Plan to use it up as soon as possible. The same with vegetables and potatoes. Make stock out of leftover fish, meat, or bird bones and use it later for soups, stews or gravies.

If you have fresh fruit that seems to be going uneaten, like apples, pears, or oranges, peel, core and cut them up, sprinkle on a little sugar and a splash of brandy or Grand Marnier, mix and refrigerate. It makes a great dessert. Add bananas that may be getting browner than looks appetizing. They'll discolor pretty quickly though, so use them up as soon as possible. The juice of half a lemon squeezed over a bowl of freshly cut fruit will retard discoloration for a bit.

I always plan to have leftover potatoes; boiled they're a natural for home fries, hash, omelets, etc., and mashed, they make a cover for Shepherds Pie. Here are some recipes that will get you started. After that it's up to you, your imagination, and whatever ingredients you have left over.

VENISON HASH

Leftover deer meat, elk, turkey, pheasant...all of it makes great hash, served with fried or scrambled eggs, toasted English muffins, and Bloody Marys. 'Tis a fine way to start the day.

    1 lb. cooked venison ground or diced very small
    4 or 5 medium potatoes, cooked and diced
    1 large onion, diced
    ½ tsp. thyme
    ½ stick of butter
    salt, pepper, Tabasco sauce

Melt the butter in a large skillet over medium-high heat, add the venison, potatoes, onion, and thyme. Add pepper and salt and a few dashes of Tabasco. Mix and fry until it begins to brown. You may need to add a little more butter or cooking oil to help hold it together. Serve when browned.

MOCK GOOSE PATÉ

This is another good recipe from Doug Ensor of Newport News, VA.

small portion of leftover goose or duck, washed of any gravy
1 stalk celery
1 onion
pepper, salt, mayonnaise

Run the meat, celery and onion through a meat grinder, add pepper and salt to taste, mix mayonnaise until you get the right consistency for spreading on crackers or toast points.

VENISON PATÉ

2 or 3 slices cooked deer liver
1 onion, sliced
1 stalk celery, chopped
½ stick butter
1 oz. Cognac, brandy, or bourbon
pepper, salt, white wine

Wash the liver clean of any butter, bacon fat, etc. that it may have been cooked in. Run it through a fine grinder, twice if necessary. Sauté the onion and celery in the butter and brandy, and a small splash of white wine, until the onion is soft, but not brown. Mix the ingredients, including all the pan drippings, into as fine a paste as you can. If it needs moistening, add mayonnaise. Refrigerate, then serve with crackers during the attitude adjustment hours.

FISH SALAD

Trout, salmon, bluefish, sea bass, all are good in a cold salad the next day.

1 lb. leftover fish, boned and cut in small pieces
4 stalks celery, chopped
1 large onion, chopped
pepper, salt, paprika, mayonnaise

Mix all ingredients, using enough mayo to hold it together. Line a serving platter with fresh, crisp lettuce leaves. Spoon the salad onto the leaves. Garnish with cold hard-boiled egg quarters and sweet gerkins. Sprinkle with paprika.

FISH AND MACARONI SALAD

1 pkg. elbow macaroni, cooked as directed
1 lb. leftover fish, boned and cut up
2 medium onions, diced (preferably red)
2 stalks celery, diced
½ green pepper, diced
1 pinch basil
1 tsp. curry powder
pepper, salt, mayonnaise

Strain the macaroni through a colander or strainer and place in a large mixing bowl. While it is still hot, add the rest of the ingredients and mix thoroughly. Blend in the mayo...it takes a lot, until you get the consistency you want. Cover and refrigerate for several hours. You may want to add more mayonnaise before serving.

JAMBORTA

This is a kind of Italian omelet with damn near everything in it; leftover meat, potatoes, and zucchini, fresh onion and peppers, almost anything you have in the fridge or bin will work. It's fun to cook and eat, and though it's a tad heavy for breakfast, it makes a fine lunch or supper dish with hunks of Italian or French bread and plenty of wine.

½ lb. cooked meat, sliced or cut in cubes
3 or 4 cooked potatoes, sliced or diced
3 or 4 cooked zucchini squash, sliced
1 raw onion, sliced
1 green pepper, diced
1 pinch each parsley, basil, oregano
6 eggs, lightly beaten with a little milk, pepper and salt to taste, butter or oil for sautéing, grated Parmesan cheese.

Sauté the onion and pepper until the onion is soft. Add the meat, potatoes, squash, whatever you have that's cooked, and the spices. Stir frequently and fry until heated through. Add a little more butter or oil if necessary to keep from sticking. Pour in the egg mixture and stir constantly until the eggs are cooked but still soft. Spoon onto a hot platter, sprinkle with pepper and grated cheese.

SHEPHERDS PIE

A hot Shepherds Pie is a great way to finish up leftover stew or pot roast. When I was growing up during the Depression, and doing something decent with leftovers was an economic necessity, they were frequently served in our house. This recipe calls for lots of mashed potatoes, so if you don't have them leftover, it's worth making a mess of them just for this dish.

If you're using leftover stew, you're pretty much set. If you are going to use leftover pot roast, cut the cold meat up in bite-sized pieces, and you might want to thicken the gravy a bit. If gravy is in short supply, make some more.

Put the meat, vegetables and gravy in a fairly deep oven roasting pan. Skim off any congealed fat. Cover with an inch-thick layer of mashed potatoes. Sprinkle on a little cracked pepper, parsley, or paprika, and a little grated Parmesan or cheddar cheese. Dot with butter and place in a 325 degree oven. Bake until all is heated through—about 40 minutes—and the potato crust has turned a light, golden brown. If it hasn't browned the way you'd like it, pop it under the broiler for a few minutes.

ACKNOWLEDGMENTS

Sincere thanks are due to many people who provided help, inspiration, research, recipes and moral support throughout the preparation of this book;

- to M.F.K. Fisher, who was my divine inspiration, even if the result was something less than that,

- to good friends like John Kayser, Bev Gipson, Jack Mannion, Gloria Schmidt, Bob and Jack Lamson, Bill Werkner, Ed Baruth, Kay Kerr, Doug Ensor and others who gave or sent me recipes that were favorites of theirs, and often lent me their enthusiasm when mine was failing,

- to old, faithful hunting and fishing companions like Wally Bennett, Jim Piccione, Jim Brown, John Quigley, my brother Mark, and son J.T., who were so often there, sharing the experiences and memories that are the real meat and potatoes of this book,

- to Diane Ostmeyer, friend, neighbor and computer operator extraordinaire, who bailed me out over and over when my new PC inexplicably devoured great hunks of manuscript, or otherwise threatened to defeat me,

- and finally to my friend, hunting companion of many years, photographer and editor, Don Carl Steffen, and his associate Lisa Cain Curran, without whom there would be no book, and who believed in the project and in me from the very beginning.

My sincere thanks, deep appreciation and love to all.

J.J.H.

VIRGINIA COUNTRY'S
ALL NEW

HOW TO COOK A DEER ... AND OTHER CRITTERS

Sections on wine, spices, equipment, on being camp cook ...
Recipes for deer, elk, big horn sheep, upland game, fish ...

THE MOST UNUSUAL WILD GAME COOKBOOK
EVER WRITTEN!!!
Only $14.95!

(Plus $2.00 handling & postage)

Clip and send with payment to:
"Critters"
% VIRGINIA COUNTRY
PO BOX 798
BERRYVILLE, VA 22611

Or Call Toll-Free 1-800-688-8990

Yes! to How to Cook a Deer and Other Critters
Send ___ copies to me: And send one as a gift to:

Name _____   Name _____

Address _____   Address _____

City _____   City _____

State/Zip _____   State/Zip _____

Payment enclosed ☐   Amex/Master/Visa ☐

Card # _____ Exp. Date _____

Signature _____